Elise,
I hope this next year goes better for you. Enjoy college, b[illegible] do not, I repeat, marry a boy from Iowa unless he's willing to move this way!

Cancer Is A Funny Thing

A Humorous Look at the Bright Side of Cancer...
And There Is One

Love you

By Marie de Haan

6/1/2012

Elise K.

The names of the author's caregivers have been changed to protect their privacy.

Cancer Is A Funny Thing: A Humorous Look at the Bright Side of Cancer… And There Is One

By Marie de Haan

1. Biography & Autobiography : Personal Memoirs 2. Health & Fitness : Diseases - Breast Cancer 3. Religion : Christian Life - Inspirational

ISBN: 978-1-935953-06-7

Cover design by Lewis Agrell

Printed in the United States of America

Authority Publishing

11230 Gold Express Dr. #310-413

Gold River, CA 95670

800-877-1097

www.AuthorityPublishing.com

I dedicate this book to my family:

My husband
Ken

&

My children
Adriana, Michael, & Jonathan

Thank you for the privilege of living in the same household.

I thank God every day for each one of you.

I have learned, in whatsoever state I am,
therewith to be content.

Philippians 4:11b

Chapter One
The Diagnosis

As I sat on the piano bench, teaching little Anna how to run up and down the B major scale with her nimble fingers, I resisted the urge to grab my right boob and yell, "Ow, ow, ow!" at the top of my lungs.

Probably not the most professional way to act.

I shoved my long, blond bangs out of my eyes, breaking into a cold sweat. My breast had hurt for two solid days and I was about to go off the deep end.

March 19, 2009, I wrote at the top of Anna's notebook. "Anna, I want you to practice this scale with your left hand this week, okay?" I said through clenched teeth, while her mother, Karin, watched on—oblivious to my torment—in her customary station on the rocking chair next to the piano.

* * *

I had found the lump seven months earlier, in August.

"Hey, Ken," I asked my husband one night, "do you think this is anything?"

"Hmm, it sure is." He raised his eyebrows. I knew that look in those deep, brown eyes.

"I'm serious. I found this lump."

"I don't know. Let me check it out." He nestled his face into my chest.

This wasn't going anywhere. Not the way I thought it would, anyway. Of course, he thought it was going somewhere.

"Do you feel it?"

"I sure do." His hand groped my breast.

What was I asking him again? Oh, yes. The lump. I tried to guide his hand to the spot, but he couldn't feel it at all. I could barely feel it myself.

After seven months of inactivity, I finally decided to be responsible and get a routine pap smear and breast examination.

"Well, you're right, it's probably just a cyst," Dr. Morrison said, observing my insides up on his screen. He frowned.

"It sure hurts," I answered. "What would you do? Surgically remove it? Lance it?" I felt a shiver go up my spine at the word "lance."

"I think I'm going to send you for a diagnostic mammogram."

Before I knew it, I found myself not only getting a

mammogram, but an ultrasound and an extensive biopsy in rapid succession.

Over the next couple of days, I called Dr. Morrison's office for the results of my tests and kept getting the runaround. I wanted the cyst taken care of as soon as possible. Our family was leaving for California and I wanted to be able to heal from the outpatient procedure enough to be able to ride the roller coasters at Knott's Berry Farm.

By Friday, I couldn't wait any longer. This time, I would show up in person and not leave until I had my answer. My 16-year-old daughter, Adriana, sat out in the car waiting, while I marched inside. We both should have been at home packing.

"So, have you heard anything yet?" I asked at the front desk, not quite succeeding in keeping the anger out of my voice.

The receptionist stared at me with a blank look on her face. A nurse walking by, however, saw me and asked, "Oh, did they tell you about the MRI appointment?"

I shook my head.

"We made an appointment for you on the fourteenth of April."

"Fourteenth of April? I've told this office several times that I won't be here then. I'm parking my butt on the beach in California." I looked at my watch. "In fact, we're leaving in three or four hours. You're confusing me with another patient."

"Maria Ann de Haan?"

"Yes." I was losing patience.

"We have you down for an MRI at the hospital."

"What for?" This woman was obviously very confused.

She whispered in my ear, "Maybe you better come back here."

I was annoyed because they hadn't returned any of my phone calls, but had all the time in the world to set up MRIs for me when I was going to be out of town. They weren't listening to me.

I followed the nurse down the hallway to a little office and sat down.

"Dr. Chen will come and talk to you."

"I normally see Dr. Morrison."

"Well, Dr. Morrison is out right now and Dr. Chen will talk to you instead."

Waiting, waiting, waiting. This cyst was bloody interfering with my life.

Adriana, still out in the car, was probably wondering what in the world had happened to me.

I was herded down to another room, the same one where Dr. Morrison had performed his exam ten days earlier.

Dr. Chen was a short, Chinese man who didn't look to be any older than 20. He handed me a thick stack of papers and said, with no preamble, "You have advanced breast cancer."

"Pardon me?"

"Advanced." His accent was pretty thick, but I heard that word loud and clear.

I looked down at the pathology report in my hand. These words might as well have been written in Chinese, his language, for all the sense they made to me. I honed in on the first one. "What does 'invasive poorly differentiated ductal carcinoma with abundant necrosis' mean?" I asked Dr. Chen, calm as can be.

"Advanced."

"How about 'poor tubule formation 3/3, high nuclear grade 3/3 and low mitotic rate 1/3'?"

"Advanced."

This guy was starting to tick me off. *Pick a new word already.* "Nottingham Grade. I don't know what that is. It says I have 2 out of 3."

"Advanced."

I didn't cry at all, because I didn't believe he knew what he was talking about. It was a cyst. There had to be some kind of mistake.

Realizing I wasn't getting anywhere, I stood up. Dr. Chen followed me out to the receptionist's desk.

I think he was waiting for me to break down into hysterics and when I didn't react in a typical fashion, he patted me awkwardly on the shoulder, and went about his merry way.

I asked the receptionist who I had to call to cancel my MRI appointment and went *my* merry way out to the car.

"Well, what did the doctor say?" Adriana asked me, clearly petrified to hear the answer.

"Apparently, I have *advanced* breast cancer." I couldn't get over the fact that he must have said that word about seventeen times.

My daughter burst into tears.

I still couldn't cry and snapped into practical mode. "Well, we can go home and tell the family or we can go to Fred Meyer and pick up lunch meat to put on sandwiches."

She sniffled and looked at me like I was crazy.

When she didn't answer, I broke it down for her again: "Go home or sandwiches?"

"Uh... I don't... *sniff, sniff*... know..."

"Let's get some turkey."

I must have been in shock. I still haven't really figured out why I reacted the way I did except that I'm a pretty down-to-earth person, we *were* going on vacation for a few weeks, and I wanted to make sure we had food in the car. What can I say? That's just the way I am. I didn't have time to fall apart now, advanced breast cancer or not.

At home, Ken and I disappeared into our bedroom while Adriana holed up in her room to hide her swollen eyes from her brothers.

"The doctor—some young guy about 20—said that I have advanced breast cancer."

Ken wrapped me in a big hug.

"Do you think we should cancel our road trip?" his muffled voice asked from somewhere in the vicinity of my armpit.

I pulled away. "Are you kidding me? No way. You know how much I love California. I've looked forward to this trip for over a year. We're going. We can sit and be sad here at home or we can sit and be sad at the beach. What's to think about?" I love Washington state, but the rain was getting to me.

"Mer, at least call Joe and see what he says before we hop in that car, okay?" he responded, referring to the naturopath I had seen for years.

"I will, but we're going on this trip," I said firmly. "But we do have to tell the boys now."

We called them into the living room. Thirteen-year-old Jonathan cried on my shoulder while we both sat on the couch. Fifteen-year-old Michael held it in like me, stood up quickly, and slipped into his room. Ken followed him.

I next dialed my friend Tami, whom I had nicknamed Vern back in ninth grade. "Hey, Vern, how's it going?"

"Well?" She told me later that she knew the minute I called that it was bad news.

"I have advanced breast cancer."

Ten minutes later, Tami was standing in front of me.

"I still can't believe it," she wailed as she hugged me tight.

"That makes two of us, sister," I agreed.

When we pulled apart, I looked down.

"Vern, where are your shoes?"

"I left them at my mom's. I left my wallet, too. The second we hung up, I had to come right over here."

Oh boy, it looked like my greatest friend in the world was taking it harder than me. I would have to hold her up.

"I still can't believe this is happening."

"Vern, this is the way it is. We'll get through this."

Tami went to pick up her shoes and wallet from her mom's; Ken and I threw our three kids and the turkey sandwiches into the car and drove down to Angels Camp, California in a daze.

* * *

In the condo, resting after our 18-hour drive, I sat on the couch with my feet up. The kids rested for about five minutes and then left for the outside pool with their bathing suits on and towels in hand.

Ken sidled up to me. "Hey, Mer, what are you doing?" He looked like he had been sucker-punched.

"Sitting here pretending my life is still normal." I moved my feet.

He plunked down on the couch next to me and asked, "Have you thought of journaling? It might help you through this."

"I don't want to write about cancer. I'm going to keep pretending I don't have it."

"At least write down some stuff in case you decide to write a book about it later. You just bought that laptop."

"You mean for that silly novel I wrote that will never see the light of day?" I heard the desperation in my voice, but I couldn't stop myself. "A book about cancer. Are you nuts?"

"You never know."

"Ken, I don't want to write a book or journal or anything else about having cancer," I snapped at him. "Just because I'm a writer doesn't mean I need to talk about it all the time or let other people know what I'm thinking. I still can't believe it's true."

"I know, neither can I," Ken replied. "I'm still in shock and keep thinking that I'm going to wake up one of these mornings and it's all going to be a bad dream, but it *isn't*."

"I don't feel sick. How can I have cancer? I eat all that health food. Walk for miles every other day. Use that Total Gym. Total bunch of hooey. What good did it all do me?"

"Just think about what I said, Mer, about taking notes."

"It's taken everything I've got just to get through all

these mammograms and biopsies. The medical stuff is only going to get worse when we get home." I tried not to think of bald heads and the inside of a toilet. Against my bidding, a vision of Campbell Scott in the movie *Dying Young* came to mind.

"I know."

"The subject's over. I don't want to talk about it anymore." We were on vacation, for Pete's sake, and were supposed to be having fun.

If only we had known about all the medical insurance problems awaiting us back in Washington, we might have stayed in California.

* * *

Back at home, in the land of reality, Ken and I sat in the lobby of Dr. Williamson's office, the breast cancer specialist that my naturopath, Joe, recommended. Adriana and Michael had wanted to stay home. Jonathan sat with us and read his book, *Twilight*, while we pored over the fine doctor's résumé.

"Look, he's been on 20/20 and ABC News," Ken pointed.

"Great. Cha-ching. This is going to cost us a fortune," I whispered.

While Jonathan continued his book out in the lobby, Ken and I were ushered into Dr. Williamson's office. I surreptitiously counted his diplomas. There were 14 of them.

Dr. Williamson had white hair and a bushy mustache. His kind brown eyes appraised me from the other side of the room.

“Well, Maria, let’s go over the pathology report,” he advised.

I swear, if he said “advanced” one time, I would go through the ceiling.

“What does poorly differentiated mean?” I asked him.

“It means that your cells, particularly the breast cells, are totally different from a normal cell.” He got out a piece of paper and proceeded to tell us—for *three hours*—all about breast cancer while Jonathan probably wondered if his parents had entered the Twilight Zone.

Maybe we had.

I felt like my brain was going to explode from information overload. About the only words that really stuck out in the whole conversation were: Mastectomy. Scheduled for May 12.

Dr. Williamson decided that I needed another test, an MRI, to make sure that nothing was missed on the first three tests I had done—the mammogram, ultrasound, and stereotactic biopsy.

Erg.

On May 8, Ken and I returned to Dr. Williamson’s office. I was nervous because the mastectomy was looming in four short days and I wanted to ask the big kahuna to help me decide whether or not to do reconstruction. Before I could ask my question, though, Dr. Williamson told us that the surgery would be cancelled and I would now need to do chemotherapy right away.

“What?” My heart sank. All the emotional ups and downs of deciding whether or not to a) chop my boob off, b) replace it right away with a fake one, or c) ignore it all and do nothing, and now we were discussing chemo already? The Twilight Zone just kept on coming.

"According to this latest pathology report, your cancer is now considered locally advanced—Stage III—and the most dangerous thing is not the cancer in your breast, but the spread of it to your lymph nodes." He pointed to the x-ray of my right breast and armpit.

"The first report said I have a Nottingham Grade of 2 out of 3," I said. "Now, this one says 7 out of 9. I'm still not really sure what that is."

"Well, Maria, I'd say that you really have 8 out of 9 or 9 out of 9. The Nottingham Grade is a tool that we use to measure the prognosis and the severity of your cancer."

Holy crap. Here I had sweated all week about whether or not I should do reconstruction. Now, this doctor was telling me I was toast.

On May 12, four agonizing days later, instead of getting my mastectomy done as previously planned, I sat in the waiting room with Ken for the technician to photograph my liver to see just how burned a piece of toast I really was.

I tried to calm my stomach. The Barium lunch I had consumed along with the Barium snack was making me feel like I had eaten three pizzas for lunch.

Ken tried to read the *ESPN* magazine to me. I tuned him out.

The front door to the waiting room opened and a gray-haired man shuffled through the opening and stood there uncertainly as his eyes adjusted to the dimmer light inside.

A woman three chairs down from me hustled to her feet. I looked up in surprise. The old bird was pretty spry for her age. She clunked past us with her walker, the oxygen tank trailing behind her.

The gray-haired man shrank back when he saw her stomping toward him.

"You're half an hour late!" the woman barked at him, not worrying about the fact that the waiting room was full of people.

"I've been out in the parking lot for half an hour," he replied sourly.

"Where?" she demanded.

They continued to argue on the way out the door. "I've been here waiting… well, I've been there waiting…."

I turned to my husband and said, "Promise me you'll just come right in and get me."

The young man next to me snickered.

"Ken," I whispered fiercely, "hand me that piece of paper." We already had a huge folder stuffed full of papers from this whole cancer business.

"Which one?" he answered.

"Any of them. Quick." I snapped my fingers. I found a pen in my purse and furiously tried to recapture the funny moment down on the back of one of the pages of the pathology report. Maybe I could journal about this trying time after all. If it didn't turn into a book one day, at least I'd have an interesting scrapbook to show Ken and the kids.

The three of us—Ken and I and the snickering young man—watched through the floor-length window as the old couple continued to berate each other on the way to their car.

"My goodness, I don't know if I want to get old," I said to the two of them. Then again, just after being handed a diagnosis of advanced breast cancer, I knew I wanted to live a little longer than age 42.

Chapter Two
Heal Me, Lord

I rolled out of bed, still feeling out of sorts. Cancer was exhausting.

I missed the rolling hills of Angels Camp—even the Moaning Caverns where I had a claustrophobic attack at the opening to the pit—the hot sun in Indio, the log ride at Knott's Berry Farm, and the beach and Ruby's Diner in Oceanside.

What I didn't miss were the doctor appointments. I loathed them already.

Ken and I didn't go on dates anymore. We went from liver tests to bone tests to brain tests, trying to figure out what had happened to us seemingly overnight.

I was glad Ken, a commercial real estate appraiser for a

local bank, could be at work today, to get away from me for a while. Adriana, Michael, and Jonathan were trying their best to get through their final exams at Mount Vernon Christian in spite of the new upheaval at home.

After a quick shower, I threw on some sweats and made myself a cup of Earl Grey tea. I instantly thought of my friend, Melissa. We almost always enjoyed a cup of Earl Grey tea when we got together, with or without rhubarb cake or pumpkin muffins. I picked up the phone and called her.

"Hey, Melissa, how's it going?"

"Maria. How are you feeling?"

It was the first time we had talked since the diagnosis.

"I'm doing okay. Still in shock, I think."

"I cried for ten whole minutes when I heard the news," Melissa replied.

"You did?" I didn't mean to sound so shocked. We had, after all, been good friends for over 26 years. Of course she was worried about me.

"You know what else? Every night at the dinner table, Rick will be halfway through our prayer and Isaac will belt out, 'And heal Maria!' and then start eating."

I could envision Isaac with his 6-year-old fingers clasped together and his bright blue eyes open, not closed in reverence—he was too busy to get on with his life—his little body bouncing on the dining room chair while his father completed their family grace.

"That's so cute, Melissa. I'm going to hug that kid the next time I see him."

"He says it every prayer. Hasn't missed a single one since he heard about you getting sick."

"Listen, Melissa. I've got to go. I have a drum lesson here in a few minutes."

"I didn't know you took drum lessons."

"I don't. Michael does. Or he used to." My son Michael and her son Nathan had been best friends since second grade.

"I don't understand."

"I know. It's complicated, but I really have to run or I'll be late. Tell Isaac to keep praying. I need all the help I can get."

I made it to the drum lesson within half an hour. I was excited to forget cancer for awhile and get back to something I loved to do: songwriting. I had been to more doctor appointments in the past month than I had in the three years prior to that.

Fresh out of high school, I had elected to skip college and began working at a local insurance firm. After 20 years of working up the ranks from file girl to insurance agent, switching to part time when I had babies, I made the choice to quit altogether about six years ago and teach piano lessons, a decision I never once regretted.

Late at night, after the family had gone to bed, I would go to my used Cable-Nelson grand piano, purchased with my hard-earned piano lesson money, and compose music the old-fashioned way, with pencil and manuscript paper.

"Hi, George." I shook the drum teacher's hand.

"How's it going, Marie?"

"I'm great." I rushed on, not wanting to talk about cancer. "It's too bad Michael couldn't continue his lessons with you. I know he really enjoyed them. First, there was basketball. Then, a one-week break and he jumped right into track season. I'm thankful he's so into sports, though, so at least he bypassed you for something good."

"Sometimes these things happen. Don't worry about it. So, what do you have for me?" he asked, a warm smile on his face.

"Well, I composed this song... oh, I don't even know when... a few months ago, maybe. I've got most of it done, anyway."

He took the photocopy of my composition and glanced over it.

"I took the hymn 'Now, Thank We All Our God,'" I explained further, "and then added a chorus in between verses. I'd like you to play the drums while I play piano." I indicated the keyboard he had tucked in between the three sets of drums he owned.

"Okay, this will be fun."

His voice was so soothing. Maybe I could come here again and take lessons from him—in playing the drums *and* calming my high-strung nerves.

"Say, George, I don't know if drums will even sound good with it or not. I guess that's why you're the teacher and I'm not."

He took his place behind one of the drum sets while I sat in glorious stupor in front of the piano. I hadn't touched one in over a month.

I played the introduction. George picked up his drum sticks and started softly tapping away. We were really going now. I went from triplets, to eighth notes, to sixteenth notes, and George accompanied me; we sounded great together.

For the first time in a month, my brain was not consumed with thoughts of cancer and dying. This had to do with *me*, my innermost soul and how happy it made me to be able to do something that I really loved.

Within ten minutes, we were done. George noted down on the photocopied composition four different patterns for the unknown person who would play them (those funny symbols meant nothing to me). Maybe Michael could play them if he ever got back to his drum lessons.

"Marie," George observed, "we should play this sometime for church. It really is a nice piece. I like how you did that."

Life was good. I was so happy to be playing again instead of having my liver, bones, and brain tested for cancer in addition to my right breast.

George stretched his arms while I remained on the piano bench.

"Well, I called my sister," he said. "You know, the one who had breast cancer? She lives in California."

I groaned inwardly. I know he meant well. He also wasn't the first. Sadly, everyone and their brother—okay, well, maybe sister or second-cousin once-removed on their mother's side—has had breast cancer. It was just that, today, I was a composer and happy person, not a cancer person.

Here this kind man that I had only met eight times earlier (two months' worth of drum lessons) was going to bat for me and spending money to call his sister. I listened but resolved that I was *not* going to call some stranger to discuss cancer.

What I really wanted to do was rewind my life to "before cancer" and go back to California with my family for a real vacation. I would ride roller coasters until I dropped and eat French fries and funnel cakes.

I thanked George profusely and pretended that I would call his sister.

In the Honda, I put my binder of music in the back seat and backed out of his driveway. *Remember the music. Forget about the other poor woman with cancer. You're a normal person today. Hang on to this important detail.*

Great. I was starting to talk to myself like a crazy person.

The next thing I knew, I had driven to church and made my way to the office of Randall, the music director. George had told me that the song was really good and I wanted to hold onto that.

"Hi, Randall, how are you?" I noticed he had cut his dark hair since I'd last seen him and spiked it a bit on top with gel. It was on the tip of my tongue to tell him he looked much better with shorter hair, but I didn't want him to take it the wrong way.

"Marie, it's great to see you. How are *you*?"

Once again, I hurried the conversation along, bypassing any talk of cancer, and cut to the chase.

"I just met with George. He's played drums for Bethany Covenant a few times."

"Of course."

"Anyway, he and I just went over a new composition of mine. I also wanted to look at the Finale program you have on your computer and see if it's something that I might finally break down and buy since I'm still using that outdated $40 software. Only if you have time, though."

"Sure, you can look at my computer a minute." He shuffled a few papers on his desk and rolled his chair over so that I could see the computer screen.

"Do you still have 'I Will Give You Praise' in there?" I pointed. Randall had spent a great deal of his time fixing another score of mine and making it look more professional with Finale; not only did he fix it, he ended up teaching it to the church choir and performing the piece at the Tulip Festival with a local violinist and flutist.

I had coveted the software ever since.

"Yes, I still have it here." He opened up the screen and there was the piece of music I had spent countless months on because I wrote it all out by hand with pencil before entering it into my limited software program.

"If I wanted to change the separate ledger lines, how hard would that be to do?" What would take me hours took him a few seconds and a flip of a button to fix.

"Six hundred dollars."

I sighed. "Jumping from $40 to $600 is quite a leap, isn't it?" *Especially with the medical bills I'm accruing.*

"Yeah, but you need to get it so that our computers can talk to each other, Marie. Besides, I want to buy the upgrade." He grinned.

"So, if this composition I went over with George was something we could use in church, I could email it to you, and both versions would be compatible."

"Yep."

Oh, life was looking up.

Randall and I could talk about Finale and composing—something we both loved to do—for hours, but sooner or later,

I would need to go home and feed the troops. They wouldn't be as amused about $600 programs, drum lessons, and praise music as I was. They would want dinner and step lively.

The minute I arrived at home, I picked up the phone, ordered the $600 software, and resolved to get on with my life.

Chapter Three
I've Misplaced My Underwear—or Was It My Brain?

Apparently, taking Vicodin causes more than constipation, addiction, and strange dreams. It can cause a person to lose her underwear.

It was June 3, two months since my diagnosis, and I was supposed to see the surgeon, Dr. Williamson, at 3:00.

Tami came with me, wearing shoes this time, so that we could pretend that we still had a normal friendship, one that didn't involve trip after trip to appointments that revolved around "stupid, stupid cancer" as she liked to call it.

We sat in the chairs across from the smart doctor.

"Well," he advised, "tomorrow I will be inserting the portacath." He leaned back, reached behind his chair, and took out a chart. He held it up so that we could both see.

He was getting ready to explain the procedure when he placed the placard down on his lap and said, "By the way, did you know that the portacath used to be called a 'totally implantable venous access system' and was later changed to the portacath because the company that developed them used a portmanteau of the two words 'port' and 'catheter' to show the..."

I should add that Tami and I had been sitting in Dr. Williamson's office for over an hour and a half already, listening, asking questions, starving, and we were now late for a baby shower, to boot.

As he droned on and on, I wanted to stand up on my chair and yell at the top of my lungs, "Who gives a rip what it's called, who developed it, and why? Tell me what time to flippin' be there tomorrow morning and let's get this little surgery over with."

"... the portacath is a device that is surgically inserted under the skin in the upper chest or in the arm..."

I was beginning to wonder if that portacath was ever going to get inserted anywhere, or if the doctor's history lesson was ever going to end.

"... the catheter runs from the portal, and ideally, the catheter terminates in the superior vena cava, just upstream of the right atrium. This position allows infused agents to be spread throughout the body quickly and efficiently..."

Efficiency. Hey Doc, maybe I could have fast-forwarded a video in the lobby about all this stuff I don't care about?

My stomach grumbled. I looked at Tami, pleading with my eyes and saying telepathically, "How should I get him to shut up?"

She telepathically answered me back, "I have no idea."

When the appointment mercifully ended with Dr. Williamson telling me to be at the surgery center at 6:00 a.m. sharp the next day, we finally escaped to the parking lot.

"Man, I thought that was never going to end," Tami complained.

"Stupid, stupid cancer," I said.

The next morning, I yawned. I had been yanked out of bed at 4:30 by Ken, who was only slightly less tired than I was.

We met with the woman at the front desk of the surgery center—I think her name was Joann. She asked for my insurance card. Why wasn't I being carded for having a margarita instead? I could sure use one. I know Ken was right behind me and could use six margaritas.

I handed over my insurance card and she said, "Hmm."

"Don't tell me," I remarked, "the second I turn around here and go sit in my seat, you're going to consult with your fellow nursey-nurse-friends and say, 'Ah, this poor sap. She has *that* insurance company.' Am I right?"

"Yeah, pretty much."

Ken's mouth turned down into a frown. "Don't get me started on all the insurance mess." The poor guy had taken over all of the paperwork so I could concentrate on getting better.

"I'm writing a book," I said, out of the blue. I shocked myself. I wasn't sure when my short cancer journal had turned into a book, but here I was telling a complete stranger that it was so.

"Is it going to be edgy and sarcastic?" she asked politely.

She must have read my personality the minute I walked through the door.

"Yes, and there's going to be a lot of references to this insurance company from hell. I guess I can't really call them by name, can I? I'll be sued for libel." Instead of being cranky dealing with my cancer, I had subtly started to be excited about writing a book about it. Not so excited for this small surgery, though.

Ken and I were herded through to the next step.

I had blood drawn and a blanket was thrown over me. A tube was hooked up to one end (of the blanket, not my body) and the tube blew hot air into the pockets of the covering. Overtired, I was still able to crack a joke. "Hey, Ken," I said, with only my head peeking out of billowy wisps of fabric and my neck hidden from view.

"What is it?"

"I feel like the guy on *Monk*, the fat one that's always egging him on."

I yawned again for the second time that morning and tried to keep my eyes open. I wanted to be home in bed at that moment, not being blown full of hot air.

A young man came in and introduced himself as Dr. West. "I'm the anesthesiologist. Maria Ann de Haan?" He looked down at his chart.

"Yep, that's me."

"Is your date of birth 1/9/1967?"

Whenever a medical professional asks that, I always want to say, "Why? Are you going to send me a birthday card?" I never do, though, because I know it's their job to make sure that they're not performing an appendectomy on a liver or a hysterectomy on a man.

I simply nodded.

"Are you having a venous-access system implanted?"

I couldn't keep my mouth shut on that one. Several times over the past two years— before my cancer diagnosis—my thyroid had gone into hyper-drive (most likely due to stress according to the naturopath), and chose to do so again. As a result, my mind kept racing, with my mouth following close behind. "I don't know. Dr. Williamson told me it used to be called a portacath, after the name of the company that originally... uh... or did it used to be called a venous-something-something...." My voice trailed off.

Dr. West probably thought to himself, "Not only does this chick make us come in early before regular hours, but she's secretly on crack. She told us she was taking all of those vitamins, but we know the real story."

I bit my lip and longed for duct tape to keep the words from spilling out of my mouth.

Dr. West continued, "The *venous access system*. For this surgery, do you have a strong preference for whether you are put under or just under heavy sedation?"

I practically jumped out of my puffy tent. "Put me under! Way under! I don't want to feel a thing!" I should have added, "Take my thyroid while you're at it. It's making me a raving lunatic. It's so embarrassing, especially when I'm not normally like this."

He smiled and left the room.

In the operating room, a nurse introduced me to two of her co-workers, Melissa and Rebecca, right before she got me settled on the table. I saw Dr. West, ready and waiting with his sleeping drugs. Things were starting to happen too quickly.

I saw Dr. Williamson out of the corner of my eye, fiddling with some machine. I had told him sorry at the appointment the night before that I was making him come in before hours, but he teased back, “Ha, I get an extra hour of sleep than you. You’re coming in at six, but I get to come in at seven.” I really did like him, even if he was too intelligent for his own good with the history lessons about equipment.

A second before the nurse put the mask over my mouth, I held her hand back and in a moment of clarity, piped up, “I know that there’s a Melissa here, a Rebecca, and a Dr. West.”

I heard a few giggles throughout the room.

“Rebecca, Melissa, and Dr. West. I don’t know who’s who and I’m sorry about that, but I like to know people’s names. Dr. Williamson—oh, there’s another name....” The mask was over my face and I felt myself floating away on a cloud. “Rebecca....”

It felt like minutes later when “Rebecca, Melissa, and Dr. West” popped into my brain. I realized I was in the recovery room by this time and kept on talking. “Rebecca, Melissa, and... what is that taste in my mouth?”

A nurse came into my hazy, peripheral vision. I had no idea what *her* name was. Or my name. Just what does Vicodin do to a person’s brain? I was soon to find out.

The next morning, with clean underwear in my hand, I made my way toward the shower. Somehow, along the way I got sidetracked and lost them.

It would have been faster to turn around and get a new pair, if I could have made it as far as the dresser and still remembered what I came for. The only problem with that was, there was a free-floating pair of underwear lying somewhere around the house and if I didn't find it soon, the company that was coming in two days would surely find them for me.

I spent twenty minutes looking for those blasted underwear. Ticked off, I grabbed another pair from my dresser drawer and made my way back to the bathroom. After my shower, I carefully patted my arm, still sore from the portacath surgery. I wrapped the towel loosely around my body. Since the kids were at school, I decided to go back to my room and get dressed there instead of in the bathroom. I gingerly picked up my clothes from the back of the toilet and promptly dropped my *second* pair of underwear into the wet sink. "You've got to be kidding me," I muttered out loud to the pale face in the mirror looking back at me.

By this time, I was tired and in a lot of pain despite the Vicodin. I didn't feel like putting on makeup to hide how white I was. That would take at least half an hour at the rate I was going. Besides, now I had extra laundry to add to my list of duties today. I was running out of underwear.

Chapter Four
I Think I Need Medical Marijuana Already

I was feeling worn out and it was only the middle of the day. What had happened to me? I used to be able to get oodles of work done in a day. Now, I spent all of my time at the doctor. Cancer was turning into a full-time job.

It had been a week since the portacath had been placed in my body, and I still took Vicodin and Ibuprofen to combat the pain.

The kids were at school for a couple hours yet and Ken wouldn't be home until six.

I sat down on the couch and clicked the remote. It was hard to concentrate on the words coming out of the mouths of the actors on the television screen. The show *Bones* came on. I'd never seen it, but on this episode a suspect being interrogated blurted out that he "needed medical marijuana" for the anxiety attacks that he had.

My ears perked up.

Hey, I can relate to this greasy, slimy man.

Ken and I had gone to my naturopath, Joe, a week before and he joked that he could prescribe medical marijuana if I needed it.

"Hey, Joe," I had said, "you realize I missed the sixties, right? I was only three at the time and unaware that I could smoke weed."

He carried on the joke. "Well, if you want to get it now, you can. Legally."

Ken jumped in. "Wouldn't that be a hoot, Joe? See Maria stoned on pot?"

"Hello, I'm right here," I pouted.

When we got home from Joe's office, I hopped on the computer. In reply to an email from a friend in Michigan asking how I was faring, I typed, "Hi, Becky, talked to the doctor today about medical marijuana. Too bad it took cancer at the age of 42 to introduce me to the phenomenon."

Becky wrote back in a tizzy. "What kind of doctor is he? How in the world can he promote that? There are all kinds of medications that can help with nausea once you start chemotherapy."

Did I mention that my friend is a nurse?

I thought she would understand that I was only kidding. So was the doctor. That's why I love Joe. He doesn't take life too seriously.

I wrote her back and said, "Hey listen, Becky, it was a joke." I felt like telling her that maybe *she* should take some pot to take the edge off, but thought that might be a little bit snippy. "You know I'm more into things like reading, planting flowers, and burning candles," I said instead.

Speaking of candles, as *Bones* continued, I took out the new candles I had just purchased on eBay and cut the wicks down to size. The TV show didn't hold my attention for very long. It's hard to get into a new show. Now that the pothead suspect was gone, I lost interest.

I glanced at the half-empty box of candles. They sure were a pretty bright pink. I turned the box over to see what scent they were so that I could order them from eBay again if the need ever arose. Lotus Blossom, they were called.

I changed the channel and *NCIS* came on. Ah, this show I knew. Our family went on an *NCIS* bender a year back and I missed those days. I struck a match and had just started the three Lotus Blossom candles, even though it was the middle of the day, when I heard Ducky, the medical examiner, address Abby, "Hi there, Lotus Blossom."

What are the odds?

Things like this happen to me all the time.

Bored, I turned off *NCIS* and turned my short attention span to the table between me and the television. A huge stack of cancer papers sat there, waiting for me to organize them.

Right on top, I found a folder with a bunch of information on the portacath. I thought back to my appointment with Tami and the surgeon. What did he call it again?

I opened the folder. I didn't remember what Dr. Williamson called it, but the manufacturers called it a "groshung port." Out of the corner of my eye, I caught the word "alert" written on a small credit-card-sized piece of plastic.

What was I supposed to do with that thing? Attach it to my forehead on the off-chance that I was in a car wreck? Just what would happen if someone who arrived at the scene placed a defibrillator to my chest? Would my left breast, which housed the groshung port, blow up? I hope not. It's the only healthy boob I've got left.

As I continued down the stack of papers, my hand stopped. Was I supposed to be somewhere? Heck, I didn't even know what month it was.

I suddenly recalled that I had an echo heart test on Monday and a training session with a chemotherapy nurse on Tuesday. I knew there was another appointment for Wednesday, but I couldn't remember what for.

Was today Friday? My brain had reached its saturation point about two weeks earlier.

Ken and I were bombarded with paperwork and insurance problems and had arranged to have Tami and another close friend, Susie, coordinate any drivers we might need and make sure that someone was at every doctor appointment if Ken couldn't make it. One of us had to keep working.

I managed to move my heart test to Wednesday, thereby narrowing the three appointments down to two so that Tami and Susie would only have to find two drivers rather than three. After noting the dates and times in my Day Planner, I felt relieved. I *knew* it was June and that I had the right Tuesday and Wednesday noted down. Monday was now free. Maybe I could sleep in and start feeling more like myself.

I was proud of myself for getting my act together in spite of the Vicodin and Ibuprofen still floating through my system. The feeling was short-lived, however.

Saturday morning, I was lying on the couch, still in pain. The fatigue had not abated, either. Michael came up to me and plopped down on the loveseat next to me. He had bluish-tinted lips. "Guess what, Mom?"

"Mmmm..." was all I could manage to get out.

He held up the stick that had been hidden inside his blueberry popsicle and read, "What do whales eat on their—"

"Michael, I don't care about jokes right now. I don't even know my own name," I mumbled.

He plowed on anyway. "Mom, just let me ask you this one."

"Michael, please. I'm tired."

"What do whales eat on their toast?"

I sighed in exasperation and couldn't even answer because I was so out of it.

"Mom, are you still awake?"

Still no answer.

"I just want to see if you'll remember this later, okay?"

I didn't have the heart to say, "Who cares about the dumb whale?"

He blurted out, "Jellyfish! Ha ha ha ha ha. Isn't that funny?"

"Michael, I don't feel that good. Hand me that Saltine, would you?" Too much pain medication and not enough real food.

Michael was too busy laughing at his own joke to notice that I wasn't finding it as funny as he was.

I thought over my stressful week, having the port inserted and getting strung out on Vicodin and Ibuprofen. I also thought of the appointment with Joe where Ken and I had discussed with him how I could legally obtain marijuana.

I thought, *Maybe I need to go get me some.* Not for nausea, but for this new stress in my life known as cancer.

Chapter Five
Tender Mercies and Timely Blessings

I sat in the church pew, stoned on Vicodin.

Randall was really cranking on the organ—Prelude in C by Bach, one of my favorites. The second the music stopped, though, I groaned in pain. Quite loudly. As if that wasn't bad enough, I groaned again a minute later. The Vicodin wasn't cutting it this morning.

Ken and Adriana looked at me. "Would you just shut up?" I could read on their faces, plain as day.

The summer wool I was wearing was making me itch, and I squirmed. Pastor Kent started preaching and my mind wandered. Normally, I have no problem listening to such a great minister, but today, there was no hope for me.

I daydreamed about the music studio I wanted. I guess

the drum teacher's compliments the week before about my composition had gone to my head. Not only did I just spend $600 on music software, here I was wanting to spend thousands of dollars on a recording studio. I also knew who I wanted to build it for me.

Rich was a good family friend. He had constructed a wall for me to separate the room with my Cable-Nelson grand piano from the laundry room, and he did such a great job. It was hard to teach piano lessons with unfolded laundry staring you in the face.

I taught Rich's kids, thirteen-year-old Michaela and eleven-year-old Isaac, but had been forced to cancel their last three lessons because of the portacath and resultant agony it caused.

Pastor Kent continued to preach. I picked up the bulletin and tried to read it. I was having a hard time concentrating.

After the service, I sought out Mike and Wanda, one of my favorite older couples in the church. Wanda had recently been in a serious car accident and I wanted to see how she was progressing after my visit to her in the hospital.

Mike gave me a bear hug because I was too slow to warn him about my pain.

"Aaaah," I moaned. He stiffened.

"What is it?" he asked in alarm.

"Oh, Mike, it's no big deal. Just a small surgery. We'll have to do the Russian kiss instead of hugs this time." I kissed his left check and then his right. Wanda came up and got the same treatment. Mike walked over to where Randall stood by the organ after his postlude, and soon, the two of them were deep into conversation.

"Maria, how have you been?" Wanda asked. I sat down in the pews and she sat a row behind me.

"Tired. Adriana and I worked too hard out in the garden yesterday."

While Wanda and I were talking, Elsie, who just happens to be my neighbor, came walking up the center aisle, and I could see that she was holding a quilt in her arms that I knew was meant for me.

I felt the lump in my throat.

"I'm part of a group called the Pinheads," Elsie explained. "We meet together and make quilts for people who need them."

I began crying.

Dr. Chen had told me I had "advanced" cancer and Dr. Williamson added that I was Stage III with a Nottingham Grade of 8/9 in the past two months, and I hadn't cried once. Now, here I was, blubbering.

"We want you to use this as an autograph quilt. See the blank spots?" Elsie continued. "You bring this to chemo and people can write messages when they come to visit you."

The quilt was absolutely beautiful. It consisted of all the colors that I couldn't refrain from painting inside my house—greens and creamy white and crimson red. Not only that, it was covered with copper-colored hydrangeas, one of my favorite flowers.

I tried to wipe the tears from my eyes, but it was no use. Wanda watched as Elsie handed the quilt to me. She confronted Elsie, saying, "Hey, when I was in my accident and you brought me a quilt, it wasn't that big."

Elsie fidgeted next to me. "Uh..."

"Wanda, my butt's twice as big as yours, you little pip-squeak," I said lovingly.

I clutched the quilt the whole way home.

When I put the quilt on the back of our living room couch, it blended in perfectly with the décor. It had been made just for me, by women I did not know.

I changed out of my Sunday dress and went outside to water my front flower basket, another gift I had received, this time from Tami. Michael and Jonathan sauntered up to where I stood with the hose.

"Hey Mom, what does a whale eat…" Michael began.

"Jellyfish!" I yelled out victoriously, water spraying everywhere.

Michael's mouth dropped open. Jonathan ducked to avoid getting wet.

"What?" I addressed the shocked look on Michael's face.

"Yesterday, you… well, you were sort of out of it, Mom." Michael turned to his brother. "Jonathan, Mom's *not* retarded after all."

"Very funny, boys. You think you're pretty cool, making fun of your mother."

"Jellyfish." Michael laughed again.

Inside the house, Adriana was pensive and withdrawn. I knew stuff was piling up at school, and she still refused to talk to her friends, even after my urging. I could see she was visibly upset about the cancer and didn't really want to talk to me about it, either.

I hauled her into my bedroom and told her to sit down. "Take out a pen and piece of my writing paper," I commanded. "I'm going to need some help from you." She looked at me uneasily, but said nothing and obediently picked up a pen.

"Write this down. This is your list of things to do," I explained. "Ready? 'In the event that Adriana does not feel like doing certain items and wants to be a teenager who is *not* dealing with cancer, said child, hereinafter named AJ—a ridiculous nickname if I ever heard one when she has such a beautiful name that her mother so carefully picked out for her, but which I indulge in only during special occasions, this being one... where was I? Oh, yes, the said AJ will tell her cancer-ridden mother to take a flying leap.'"

A smile crossed Adriana's face.

"Okay, continue. 'Number One. AJ will take dictation when the cancer-ridden mother—hereinafter referred to as CRM—is unable to scribble herself because she is too tired or will have her head in the nearest toilet.'"

She laughed.

"Number Two. 'You will keep the CRM stocked at all times with appropriate writing utensils. Now that you have a Washington driver's license and a checking account due to the graciousness of your CRM, you can go to Office Max to purchase said items.'"

Gosh, it was good to see her laugh again.

The severe lack of sleep from the surgery and all the pain it caused was catching up with me. I stopped. "Adriana, I need to take a nap. Can you get me an Ibuprofen?" I asked. So much for the nice moment we were having.

I walked out to the couch and snuggled beneath the new hydrangea quilt. I had a fear of falling asleep in my own bed and waking up in excruciating pain with no one there to help me. I took the pill Adriana had retrieved from the medicine cabinet.

"Wake me up if you need me, okay?" She nodded and disappeared into her bedroom, right around the corner from the couch where I slipped into pain-free unconsciousness. The next thing I knew, Adriana was standing above me.

"Mom."

"Hm."

"Are you awake? I think you were having a nightmare."

Suddenly, I sat up. I *had* been dreaming, but I was too tired to remember what it was about—when the pain hit and strange noises started coming out of my mouth.

Adriana's eyes opened in alarm.

I tried to control the guttural sounds that kept escaping from my lips, but it was no use. I should have stopped being so paranoid about becoming addicted to the pain pills and just taken them. "Grab my legs!" I yelled.

She hesitated and I could tell what she was thinking: *What do legs have to do with anything? I thought you had breast cancer.*

"Oh, leg cramps. Help me."

I hated what this cancer was doing to my family. It was one thing to deal with my own issues, but seeing how the rest of the family suffered really bothered me.

The next morning, when Adriana came to kiss me goodbye before driving herself and her brothers to school, I could tell that she was valiantly trying to hold everything in.

I rolled out of bed, slipped into my shoes, and said, "I'm coming with you."

When we arrived at school, Michael and Jonathan ran

off to get to their respective classrooms on time. I ordered Adriana to tell me where the guidance counselor's office was. I went there while she went back out to sit in her car.

"Mr. Fikkert. Hi, I'm Adriana's mom." I tried not to think of how my hair looked and how much mascara had smeared over the bags under my eyes.

"Hello, it's nice to see you."

"Does Adriana talk to you or the other teachers here about my cancer?"

"Well, when I ask for prayer requests, Adriana will say things like, 'Be with my parents, who went to Bellingham today.' A few of my fellow teachers know, but the students do not. We're trying to give Adriana her space."

"Okay, this is what's going to happen." Where was this firmness coming from? Usually, I was a bit of a wimp.

He looked at me expectantly.

"You are going to announce to your classroom that Adriana's mother has cancer and it's okay to talk about it. Adriana's going to bring me back home. When she comes back, she'll make up any work she needs to or take any exams she's missed."

He shook my hand. "I think that's a wonderful idea."

As Adriana and I barreled down the freeway, intermittently sobbing and laughing, I told her, "You realize, right, that God gives us grace to make it through the day—just when we think everything can't get any worse and we can't take any more?"

She nodded, the tears drying on her face.

"I even wrote a title down last week in my frenzy to get the cancer journal in order." My kids were going to be so sick and tired of this book. "It was called Tender Mercies and Timely Blessings."

"Okay, Mom, I get it."

"No, I don't think you do. You can't keep holding all this fear inside of you and not talk to your friends about this stupid, stupid cancer, like Aunt Tami calls it. Did you think you were betraying my confidence to talk about it?"

"I don't know."

"Adriana, your friends can't help you through a bad situation if they don't know what's wrong. They're only human."

"I didn't want to bother them."

"If they're true friends, Adriana, they will be there for you and help you through it."

"Thanks for talking to Mr. Fikkert for me." I could see her shoulders were not quite as stooped. Mission accomplished.

Speaking of missions, I told Adriana, "We need to get home. I forgot Melissa is coming over in an hour. We're going to do some yard work. I want to get on top of stuff because my chemo-training appointment is tomorrow already." What had I just been saying about tender mercies? Here I was, complaining before I even started.

Chemo was going to be a big leap for me. I don't even use aspirin, except for very rare occasions. Now, I was popping Vicodin and Ibuprofen like they were candy, and it was getting easier and easier all the time. The next thing I knew, I'd be addicted to Vicodin and would have to write another book, *How I Became Addicted to Vicodin During Cancer Treatment While Trying to Write a Humorous Book.* Maybe too long of a title?

Adriana dropped me off at home and headed back to school. I washed my face, changed into proper work clothes, and was eating an apple when Melissa showed up.

"Melissa, how's it going?"

"Good."

"Isaac still on prayer duty?"

"Every single prayer. You'd think he'd forget or move on to something else, but he never, ever misses a beat."

"He's so sweet. So are you, by the way, for coming over here to help me with this mess." I indicated the weeds galore surrounding our house.

She put her gloves on and walked toward the front flowerbed.

"Melissa, wait. We have to do some stuff in the back first."

"Don't you want to do this front one first?"

I mean, what *normal* person wouldn't start with that flowerbed? It's the front of the house and makes a statement about a person.

What my front flowerbed says about me on a regular basis is, "My owner is a slob and has too much on her plate. Sure, she's a writer, songwriter and poet... she has good intentions always, but...."

I told the front flowerbed to shut up and dragged my well-meaning friend to the back yard where the twenty-five $2.00 Emerald Greens awaited certain death if they didn't get planted soon, and where the phlox had to be uprooted and transplanted—the phlox from her garden, in fact.

What had happened to me? I used to be so... so...

unaccepting of help and now, here I was barking out orders to Melissa like I was a drill sergeant: “No, you cannot work on that first-impression flowerbed. You must follow me to the back yard where all kinds of backbreaking work awaits us.”

Thank heavens Melissa is the way she is. She rolls with the punches.

A few hours later, we moved to the shade. While Melissa edged the grass pathway crookedly, bless her heart, I felt guilty about having this young mother of three help me in this obsession of mine, gardening.

“Hey, Melissa,” I panted from my side of the garden, “I’ll have to come to your house sometime and help you catch up on your yard work.”

“Um... Maria, my flowerbeds are all done.”

Of course they were. She wasn’t a slob like me. Yeah, but she couldn’t carry a tune or make up a 12-page choral piece with flute and violin descant, I consoled myself.

Melissa left to pick up Isaac, Alyssa, and Nathan from school. I fell asleep on the couch. Until the phone rang.

It was another friend of mine.

“Maria, I wanted to call and let you know that my husband and I talked it over and we would like to pay for half of your school tuition.”

“I can’t let you do that.”

“Stop. You let me talk for once.”

I let her talk. It was easy, because I had a big lump in my throat again, for the second time that week. First the quilt, now this.

“We know how important it is to you and Ken to send the kids to private school, and now that you have all these bills piling up, we want you not to have to worry about the tuition bill on top of everything else."

"We're talking ten grand here. That's a lot of money." I wanted to make sure there wasn't some sort of misunderstanding. Maybe they didn't know how much tuition cost.

"We know that's how much it is. We insist and want you to just have one part of your life taken care of so that you can get well."

I had to hang up because I was crying so hard.

I felt guilty about waiting so long to get to the doctor. Seven months I waited. It was *my* fault we were suddenly in this financial strait. It was *my* fault I went and got sick.

Quilts. Gardening help from friends. Cards pouring in every day. Meals provided by others. Now, tuition.

This was more than tender mercies. This was overwhelming.

Chapter Six
Pharmacy or Fishing?

I missed normal life. Hiking, going out with friends to dinner, family movie nights at home; these were things of the past.

"Hi, Ken? Maria? My name is Kateri. I'll be explaining the chemotherapy regimen to you." The three of us were crammed into a tiny, white office. The nurse got out a three-inch binder.

Crap. Just what was going to happen to my body, anyway?

Kateri went on. "Today's June 9. You'll be starting chemotherapy next Wednesday, the 17th. I'm going to walk you through some of the steps, okay?"

My mind kept wandering as she went through the

papers in her binder, holding up pictures on occasion. Toward the end of her speech, she made an offhand remark about how I needed to be careful because my immune system would be suppressed. She mentioned dirt.

"Excuse me?"

"You need to be careful if you're around dirt."

"Why in the world would I need to do that?" I asked.

"Because there are bugs in the soil."

"Duh. Ladybugs, beetles, and a whole bunch of nameless bugs. They're not really nameless, of course, I just don't know them. Personally, at least."

"They can make you sick."

Boy, medical thinking and naturopathic thinking are on opposite ends of the spectrum. During the "marijuana appointment," Joe had referred me to another naturopath, Dr. Burton, who specialized in oncology; she had told me that she thought it was great that I was into flowers, trees, vegetables, and herbs.

While I didn't plan on rolling in any pigpens or compost piles, I planned on working in the soil, what with a retail flower business and a gardening addiction to feed. There were certainly worse ways to compromise my immune system: drinking myself into oblivion, taking up smoking, doing cocaine.

"What if I wear gloves?"

"Please be very, very careful," Nurse Kateri conceded.

I held up my left ring finger and shoved the faded scar in her face. "You mean, don't try to prune off any limbs?"

Kateri cringed. Maybe I had pushed too far.

"Yeah, don't do that."

I turned to look at Ken. He looked like he had been hit by a bus. While it wasn't going to be a picnic for me, chemotherapy was going to be hard on him as well. I knew he felt helpless and scared. I didn't know how to comfort him, though, because I was trying hard myself not to think back on how chemotherapy had affected someone I loved.

My cousin Terri, one of three sisters with whom I was very close when I was younger, was diagnosed with breast cancer at the age of 26 in 1989.

When we were kids, my mom would allow me to go to Uncle Sid and Aunt Alice's almost every weekend and the four of us—Terri, Susan, Linda, and I—would play for hours on the farm where they lived.

Terri and I would alternate playing the piano while Linda accompanied us on the guitar. We would belt out "Jeremiah was a bullfrog!" from the song "Joy to the World" in gravelly voices or "The Holy City" opera-style and giggle and roll around on the floor near the piano until our sides hurt.

Terri, Linda, and I would celebrate when we finally convinced Susan, the non-game-playing person of the bunch to join our Othello tournaments or Operation game. Usually, the most we got out of her was one hand of Uno.

We'd make hay forts out in the barn or take turns riding the three-wheeler between the cows out in the fields.

The four of us grew from gangly teenagers into young women in our twenties and by the time Terri, the oldest of us by a few years, was diagnosed a decade later, she was already Stage IV.

I watched her suffer through the ravaging effects

of one chemo drug after another and go from a vibrant, cheerful, outgoing young woman to a shell of a person, and I vowed that I would do whatever it took to stay away from chemotherapy if the need ever arose.

Now, here I was, twenty-one years later, talking to a chemotherapy nurse.

The one condition I made to Ken before agreeing to chemotherapy was that I wanted to talk to a naturopath first. Dr. Burton agreed with Dr. Hoffman, the oncologist, and Dr. Williamson, the surgeon, that neoadjuvant chemotherapy (meaning chemo before surgery) was the best course of action. She would do everything in her power to help minimize the horrible side effects that Kateri had been talking about all morning.

Kateri stood up. "Ken and Maria, I'd like to show you where you will actually receive your treatments." We followed her down several hallways into a large square room with recliners scattered around the perimeter. Kateri leaned over to whisper in my ear, "I recommend grabbing the green chairs. They're the most comfortable."

"Got it." I felt the sweat beginning to drip down my back. I did not want to hang out in this room with other sick people and compare chart notes or types of cancer.

"Here's the kitchen." She pulled the folding door aside and pointed. "They have crackers, oatmeal, tea, chips, nuts."

What about a get-out-of-jail-free card?

"We can come in here and get whatever we need?" Ken asked.

"Yes, that's what it's there for."

We continued walking around the square. I tried not

to stare at the patients sitting there. *Oops, that man got a gray chair. He doesn't look very comfortable, alright, but it's probably that medicine they're pumping into his veins.*

"Do you have any questions?" Kateri asked.

"Yeah, do I really have to do this?"

"You really have to do this." She shook our hands and went back to work with other seasoned patients. Ken and I walked down the hallway. I carried my purse and camera and he carried the folder of "cancer papers."

Ken stopped in front of a large office. Two chairs had been placed to the left of the doorway. "Mer, I have to go talk to the lady in charge of the financial stuff. Do you want to stay here?"

I nodded. I felt the familiar guilt creep up my spine. Man, I was going to cost this family a fortune.

I sat down on one of the chairs and put my purse and camera on my lap. I fingered the camera bag strap and got an idea. I'm not sure why I had it with me. Sometimes when I'm feeling stressed, which lately, I definitely was, it calms me down to have it in my possession.

Back at the counter where I first checked in, I leaned my head through the open window. "Hi, my name is Marie de Haan. Kateri walked us through the chemo training a minute ago." I was talking extremely fast, a long-term nervous habit I've had a hard time correcting.

The receptionist looked at me as if to say, "And I care, why?" but she smiled anyway.

"Can I see her for just one quick minute?"

Kateri peeked her head around the corner and also smiled. She probably thought, "Get away from me, you granola freak. You can go play in the dirt now."

"Hi Kateri, Ken is down talking to the lady about all our financial woes and thanks for talking to me this morning and I really appreciate all the time that you took to talk to me and I just wanted to know if it's okay if I take your picture because I'm writing a book about this whole experience and I won't ever, ever use the picture without your permission and I don't even know if the book is going to have pictures or even be a reality, but just in case, I was wondering if that's okay?"

Phew.

I could hear how hyper I was in my own ears, but couldn't stop myself. I didn't want to do the chemo, I wanted to make sure I kept all the paperwork straight, I wanted to keep writing through this experience, and I wanted to remain *myself*. I didn't feel like myself.

Kateri was gracious. She allowed another nurse to snap two photos of us.

"Thanks again, Kateri, and I'll try to remember to grab the green chair when I come back." I wandered back out to the hallway and sat in a chair outside the financial office.

Ken finally came out and his shoulders were a bit more hunched than before he went in. This was going to kill him before it killed me.

"Where do we have to go next?" Ken asked. We headed for the parking lot.

"Fred Meyer in Burlington. We have to pick up that prescription for Emla that Dr. Williamson filled out for me, remember? That's the stuff I'm supposed to goop on the portacath site so that it doesn't hurt when they put the needle in for the *drugs*."

"They're not drugs, Mer. Well, they're drugs, but they're chemotherapy medicines that are going to save your life."

"Well, Ken, I don't want to take them," I pouted.

"I know you don't."

"I always said that I wouldn't do chemotherapy." By this time, we were sitting in the Honda. "Maybe we should find a new naturopath, one who thinks it's a good idea to forget all the drugs and do vitamins, carrot juice fasts, and parasite cleanses instead. It would be cheaper."

"We're going for a cure, here."

"It would be cheaper if I died and that life insurance kicked in."

"How can you say that?"

"Because I'm tired and don't feel like doing this."

Ken backed up and we headed toward Fred Meyer. When we arrived in the parking lot, I asked Ken, "Are you coming in with me?" I couldn't remember the last time I had a prescription filled, if ever.

"I'm going to stay here and guard the computers." He had his work laptop with him, and I had brought mine along in case I thought of something brilliant to write for the cancer book I found myself thinking more seriously about writing.

"I should be right back," I told Ken. How hard could it be to get a little tube of pain-numbing medicine?

Pharmacy, the sign read. I headed that way.

There were four signs hanging from the ceiling: "Rx Pick Up," "Rx Pick Up" (guess that was an important one since they were repeating themselves), "Consultation," and "Rx Drop Off."

Which one should I pick?

An older woman stood in line directly in front of me, looking confident that she was where she was supposed to be. The woman in front of her strode up to the counter. I stood behind both of them and the sign that said, "Please wait here for the next available line."

An aged man, very skilled with his walker, came flying up beside me. "Are you going this way?" he asked me.

I shook my head in confusion and studied the four signs again. It had been a long, stressful day at the chemo training and I was worn out. I looked down at the prescription clutched in my hand. Dr. Williamson had told me a long time ago (five whole days) to rub the Emla cream on the top of my left breast where the portacath was located, let it soak in, and put some plastic wrap over it sixty minutes before my regular chemo treatments.

I was going to drop the prescription off, but I was picking up the Emla, this tube of miraculous goodness that was going to make my life so much better. Rx Pick Up or Rx Drop Off?

Now, normally, I am a reasonably intelligent young woman, but I sat and stared at the prescription and didn't know what to do. My gaze darted from one sign, down the row to the next, over and over. My eyes settled on the sign "Consultation." By this time, I wanted to sit on the floor and cry like a baby. "I'll consult someone alright... Mommy."

I finally decided I should stay put and take my chances with the "Rx Pick Up" line. The efficient lady on the other side of the counter would tell me if I was in the right place or not. Sure enough, when I got to her, she told me that I was in the wrong line and needed to be in the Rx Drop Off line.

"Do I just walk over there?"

She nodded and motioned the next person to come up.

I moved over to the Rx Drop Off line (past the Consultation line) and handed the woman standing there my prescription. She told me it would be half an hour.

I needed a drink. Too bad I don't drink. Maybe now would be a good time to start. Instead, I escaped to the car.

"What took you so long?" Ken asked.

I resisted the urge to start bawling and answered, "It won't be done for half an hour. Let's go to Office Max with our precious thirty minutes and get the Cancer Box."

At home, we had a lot of paperwork to store and keep track of. We had one tall, metal file cabinet full of personal papers. There were also several plastic mobile file boxes with lids that I had purchased over the years to help in the endless quest to organize myself.

First, there was my TriVita Box, the file cabinet that contained my vitamin-selling business that I was devoting less and less time to because I was angry at vitamins at the moment, and swamped with doctors besides.

Second, there was my Music Box, to keep track of all the receipts, music catalogs, and forms I needed. Teaching was another thing I hoped to continue while going through chemotherapy. Visions of being halfway through a student's lesson and having to run off to the bathroom to stick my head in a toilet already embarrassed me.

Third, there was the Wayside Wisteria Box. I had started this retail nursery and gift shop back in 1999 and had hopes of starting it up again someday when I wasn't burdened with the other responsibilities in my life, the biggest one being not dying.

Fourth, I had my Writing Box, the newest of the bunch. It was full of manuscript ideas, notes I had taken at the two Whidbey Island writing conferences I had attended, and the stories I composed during the creative writing class I had taken—with a bunch of senior citizens—from a really good teacher named Ruth.

We zipped over to Office Max and found the box within minutes. It took several more minutes to talk about it, though.

"What do you think?" I asked. "It looks different than the other boxes I have."

Even Ken, who is normally direct and to the point, began to hem and haw. He lifted the box up off the shelf and began to inspect it. "What's wrong with it?"

"I don't know. It just seems different. We could go to Office Depot and see what they have but that prescription will be done pretty soon. I'm getting kind of burned out."

"We could go to Office Depot if you want."

"Don't you think we should just get this one?" I answered. "The boxes don't have to be exactly the same, do they?"

I don't know when the OCD began to set in. I liked order, but seriously, this was going beyond that. Frustrated, I grabbed the bin out of his hands. "Let's just get this one and get out of here. My brain stopped working about two hours ago."

I almost made it out of the aisle. Ken bumped into me as I stopped mid-stream. "Ken, what do you think? Do you think we should get a different one that has handles? I mean, do you think that I will actually be lugging this box into the doctors' offices or leaving it in the car?" I had enough to carry with my laptop, camera, lipstick, and worthless insurance ID card.

My goodness, we had talked with Kateri this morning about the thousands and thousands of dollars' worth of drugs that they were going to pump into my veins and I was sweating over $12.00 for a mobile file cabinet?

Back at Fred Meyer's consultation area, the kindly old pharmacist stood holding my medicine in his hand and asked me, "Prior to use?"

"Excuse me?"

"It says prior to use. Use for what?"

"Chemo, I guess. Dr. Williamson said to rub that wonder cream on this little spot here," I pointed to the purple circle on my chest, careful not to get too carried away and expose my left nipple to this man, trying to make him understand. He was confusing the heck out of me.

He wouldn't give up. "The doctor just wrote, 'Use this cream 60 minutes prior to use' on here," he tried to explain to me patiently as if I were a child. I didn't know what he wanted from me.

"Yes, yes... that's what the doctor told me. Rub that cream on 60 minutes before I get there and—"

He cut me off. "Where?"

I thought we had had this conversation already. "To the chemo treatments."

"But, prior to use," he insisted. "What does that mean?"

Our noses were practically touching by this time. Ken wandered up, holding a bag of groceries we needed, and watched our verbal tennis match.

"All I know," I reassured the man with the nice nose, "is that Dr. Williamson said to put this on before every chemo treatment. I'm starting next week. He said to use it and it wouldn't hurt."

"He didn't say that, though. It says 'prior to use,'" he repeated.

I wasn't going to get any dinner tonight.

"Dr. Williamson told me all this at the appointment the other day." *I can't help it he didn't clue you in, but I don't know what you're getting at. Prior to use makes sense to me. Prior to the chemo treatments, slather this cream on my chest, making sure to get it in the right spot or I will be in tons of pain. That's all I got out of the conversation, buddy... now, can we part noses and be done with this business?*

Somehow, we got it all straightened out. I'm still not sure what his beef was or if I understood the whole conversation, but maybe I'll have better luck next time. Ken assured me in the car that, sadly, I would be an old pro at the trip to the pharmacy before we knew it.

What I really wanted to do, though, was take a boat out into Puget Sound and go fishing. Listen to the waves lap against the boat, feel the cool breeze on my face, and forget all about my life.

Chapter Seven
Friends

Susie was a good friend.

We met when I was 18 and I started working at the insurance brokerage. I was the file girl; she was the vice president of the company. While I quit working for the firm to teach piano lessons, she didn't retire until several years later, just in time to start driving me to my appointments.

On this particular day, June 10, the day after my chemo training with Kateri, we sat in the waiting area of the Cardiovascular Center. We had wandered through the maze of St. Joseph's Hospital; it was my second or third time—I was losing count—and Susie's first, but we finally checked in and sat in the waiting area.

An older gentleman came around the corner and said gallantly, "Maria?"

I stood up and Susie followed me. The man practically bowed and said, "I will be taking you to the Fireplace Room."

"Now, there's one I haven't been in yet. Wow, a fireplace room?" I gushed. The corners of his lips curled up slightly and I almost expected to see a white towel hanging over his right arm. Next, he would be offering me crumpets. I reminded myself that I was here for an echocardiogram, otherwise referred to as an echo, not an English high tea.

The chemo drugs were hard on the heart, sometimes causing permanent damage, and Dr. Hoffman wanted to keep an eye on mine.

Susie and I sat down.

So this was the Fireplace Room. I was impressed. There were two bookshelves flanking either side of the fireplace, with healthy pothos plants creeping along the top of the shelves between the glass candle holders.

Comfortable leather couches were arranged in front of the fireplace and classy artwork adorned the walls. The cherry wood table between us held a bouquet of fresh summer flowers.

We were only in the Fireplace Room for a few minutes before a young woman came and whisked us off into the next room. This room wasn't quite as homey as the Fireplace Room, but it got the job done.

The nurse introduced herself as Brooke. "Why are you here?" she asked.

"I found a lump in my breast last August and had it checked out by the gynecologist during a pap smear several months ago."

"The gynecologist?" she asked in amazement.

"Yeah, he did his exam and then used his scope-thing to check the lump I had."

"What? He used the vaginal tool?"

"Yes."

Susie thought that was funny and laughed quietly on the other side of the room as she watched Brooke do her job.

Brooke told me to take a small breath, hold it in, let it out, and then take another deep breath, hold it in, let it out. Halfway through the small breath, I began talking. I couldn't help myself. She couldn't help herself, either. She put her hand on my arm. "Maria, you need to be quiet."

When I could talk again, I asked, "Hey, instead of looking at my boring old heart, don't you have any good movies? And don't say *Forrest Gump*. I hated that movie."

Susie continued to check the innards of my chest cavity, and exclaimed, "I can't believe it. The heart is truly amazing." We all looked up at the screen.

"I guess when you watch TV shows like *House* or *Grey's Anatomy*, Brooke, you laugh at the show because it's really fake." I breathed. "Do you watch those?"

"I don't watch *House*," she replied, "but I love *Grey's Anatomy*."

Susie started laughing. "Maria, you're the only person I know who can make friends stretched out on the table while you're having pictures taken of your heart." Ken had told me the same thing on several occasions.

"What about when George O'Malley was lying on the table and Meredith didn't know it was him?" Brooke went on, ignoring Susie.

"Yeah, and what was all that baloney about Double-O-Seven?" I asked Brooke, also ignoring Susie.

"I don't know. I think that was way earlier in the series."

Another woman came in and Brooke stood up. "I need you to take over here, Lila, because they need me in the OR." Boy, I felt like I was in a television show of my own. I wish they would find someone else to play me.

Lila wasn't as personable as Brooke. She asked me if a mammogram was how I found out about the lump.

"Yes, I had a mammogram back in March."

"I've never had one of those things," Lila volunteered.

"How old are you?" I blurted.

"Almost 52."

"Well, you better get in, then," I told her. Wasn't there something backwards here?

"Yeah, I don't want to find out anything bad," she explained. "I waited so long for boobs when I was younger. I don't want to know anything bad about them now."

We continued talking as she put the IV in my arm and stumbled upon the subject of thyroids. I told her—feeling the need to explain to everyone that I was crazy for a reason—that my thyroid was way off kilter at the moment.

"That's okay. I took a bunch of extra thyroid medication myself last night. Stayed up way too late because of it."

"That's dangerous, you know," I said, once again reversing roles. "I almost crashed the car the other day because of the extra thyroxin floating around in my system. You need to be careful."

"Oh, it's okay. I got it off the Internet."

What? First, I had impertinently asked her age, then, I told her to get a mammogram. Now I was telling her to take it easy on the thyroid meds.

I wished Brooke would come back. We seemed to click a bit easier.

Susie and I had a precious half hour before we had to be at the next appointment. "Hey, you want to zip over to Big Lots?" she asked me.

"Well, of course," I replied. "Except, I don't know how to get there. Tami does, but I still get confused up here."

Susie knew where it was, as Big Lots was one of her favorite stores. Once there, we began looking for four or five pots that she could use to put some of the $2.00 Emerald Green trees we had discovered on one of our prior shopping ventures.

I had to chuckle. Susie never used to be a gardener. She worked hard at her career; that was why she was the vice president and I was the file-girl-turned-agent. She never had the time or inclination to sit outside and dig in the dirt. I had changed all that in a hurry. Good thing her immune system wasn't suppressed.

"What do you think of that pot?" she asked me.

"Too big and 18 bucks apiece."

We looked along the whole row but couldn't find anything that would work. The pots were too big, too small, or too expensive. Next, we had to worry about the color.

"Do you think these would match the house?" Susie asked.

"What color is your house?" How could I not remember the color of her house?

"Gray."

"I think it would be nice if you could match the trim."

"The trim is off-white."

We looked but still couldn't find anything. We were getting frustrated. I turned and discovered six pots that were the perfect size, the perfect color, and the perfect price. Susie pounced on them and put them in the cart.

"Do you need anything?" she asked me.

"Yes."

She looked up in surprise. "What is it?" she asked eagerly.

"I got this plant from Tami and I love it. The only problem is it's in this square kind of pot"—I demonstrated with my hands—"but I don't have a drainage dish to go with it. I've looked everywhere. Fred Meyer, Target, Value Village." I barely had the words out of my mouth when Susie was off and running. That's how she is. She sees a need and goes in search of the answer. She's always been that way.

We went over that whole store and there was not a single square dish that would have worked with the odd-sized pot. We did, however, find a nice white cast-iron bench.

"Susie, look. You know the Cottage Garden that I have by the stand?" I was referring to Wayside Wisteria Theme Gardens, my retail nursery. "That garden has white wisteria and pale pink, white, and dusty blue flowers. This bench would be perfect in the back of that garden. I could turn that little section into a Secret Garden." I looked down at the size of the bench. "Secret Garden for one, maybe," I added.

"It would be perfect," Susie agreed.

I looked at the price tag. It was originally $120, marked

down to $65. “Do you think it’s worth that? We have all these medical bills. Getting this would be irresponsible.”

“If it wasn’t on sale, I probably wouldn’t get it.”

“I’ll want to sit out there when I’m feeling yucky from chemo, don’t you think?”

“Definitely.”

After we had packed up the pots and the bench into her vehicle, we zipped over to Dr. Williamson’s office. By the time we were done there, we were both starving. It was tiring going to two doctor’s appointments in one day.

“Hey, let me treat you to lunch,” Susie said, cheerful as ever.

“Driving me all over creation to these boring appointments is enough, Susie,” I argued.

“Oh hush.” Off we went, down toward Bellingham Bay, and landed at the Anthony’s Hearthfire Grill. We went inside and were seated by the window. Instead of looking out at the beautiful ocean view from the window, my eyes were glued on the plate that was on the table in front of me. The hunger headache I was feeling didn’t stop me, clear-headed as could be, from staring at the plate.

“Susie,” I gasped. “Look, a square plate. It’s perfect.”

She laughed her head off.

No, I did not steal that plate. I did, however, enjoy a good lunch with a great friend. Maybe I could manage to have a life and cancer all at the same time.

Chapter Eight
Bean-Counting: What's a Human Life Worth?

Friday, June 12. I sat on the couch, feet on the table, my to-do list in hand. I only had five more days before chemotherapy began, and I had a lot of things to get in order before that day.

Number One. Read those six easy-reading books that Dr. Hoffman, the oncologist, gave me over a week ago: *Understanding Chemotherapy, Cancer and You, Nutrition For the Person With Cancer, During Treatment, Understanding Radiation Therapy*, and my personal favorite, *Sexuality and Cancer*, a book I'm sure will tell me how this whole process is going to turn me into a sexless old hag at the age of 42.

Number Two. Find the copy of our last two tax returns

so that we can bring them to the advocate, Andrea, that Ken found to help with our mounting bills. That should only take me three weeks to find.

Number Three. Forget this silly to-do list and go take a shower. It's 8:30 already.

The water felt great on my hair. The hair felt great on my head. Before long, it would all fall out, according to Dr. Williamson and Dr. Hoffman.

I turned the water off, shoved the shower curtain aside, and reached around the corner for the towel. My fingers met empty air. I spied the hand towel hanging on the other side of the bathroom.

Erg.

I stepped out onto the floor, dripping water all over as I went, and bent down to retrieve a regular-sized towel out of the cupboard. The only problem was, I was met with more empty space.

"You've got to be kidding me," I groaned. I seemed to be saying this phrase a lot more lately, and out loud.

I remembered the neatly-folded towels were on the dryer at the other end of the house and had not quite made their way to the bathroom. I grabbed the hand towel, which is approximately 5 inches by 6 inches, and looked down at my body, which is definitely bigger than that; I have been overweight for more years than I care to count.

I tried to dry off as much water as possible, which was an impossible task. I glanced down at the towel and realized that this was like sending an elephant to China with a 37-cent postage stamp.

I peered around the corner in the general direction of the

laundry room. The kids were out with friends, celebrating their last day of school, which had been the week before. What I didn't remember was that the drapes in the living room were wide open. I did not want Number Four on my list of things to do before chemo to be "Get caught buck-naked by the UPS man."

I ran to the laundry room as fast as I could—past the open drapes—dripping water the whole way. I grabbed one of the folded towels off the dryer and retreated to my bedroom.

Once I was finally dressed, I sat back down on the couch.

Number Four. Answer the doorbell. What do you know? There was the UPS man. What are the odds? Am *I* glad he didn't show up fifteen minutes earlier. I'm sure he is, too; he just doesn't know it.

Number Five. Figure out where I have to be and when. I have chemo coming up and I still have a lot to do.

Ken walked into the living room and scared me. "What are you doing home from work?" I asked him.

"I didn't go to work this morning. I went for a run. What are you doing?"

"Trying to make a list of all the things we need to do before chemo next Wednesday."

"Mer, did you remember that we're meeting with Andrea at WAHA today to go over the financial stuff?"

"No. Shoot, that's today? What's WAHA again?"

"Whatcom Alliance for Healthcare Access."

"Oh yeah, number two on my list. 'Find tax returns.' I haven't found them yet and forgot that we were going there today."

"They're already in the Cancer Box."

What would I do without him?

An hour and a half later, we found ourselves crammed into the office of Andrea, our new advocate-in-this-new-mess-we've-found-ourselves-in, and she was very efficient. Ken took out the reams of statements he had been collecting over the past months and he and Andrea began to talk.

"Ken, I'm going to the car," I whispered in his ear. I couldn't take any more talk about money. I shuffled my way to the car, alone and depressed, when the word "bean-counting" popped into my brain. I had first heard this term on the movie *Class Action* with Gene Hackman and Mary Elizabeth Mastrantonio.

Bean-counting is a financial term applying to accountants who scrutinize a company's budget for forms of financial waste. In *Class Action*, it was the bean counter's job to decide what would be more cost-effective for the powerful insurance company they were representing: pay off the plaintiffs in the class action suit, or take a gamble and hope the separate lawsuits would amount to a smaller amount of money?

I was doing sudden bean-counting of my own. Should I deny all treatment and die a quick death so the family could collect life insurance? This way I would not put the family under with all these medical bills we were accruing at a rate five times faster than our income. Or should I take a gamble and try to still be an asset to society in some way?

Don't get me wrong. I love life and always have. People frequently tell me that I seem to do it all and live life to the fullest.

I recall Oprah saying one time, "Find something you

love to do and find a way to get paid for it." My problem is, I like too many things—music, food, gardening, children, and writing, to name a few. What I don't like is having money problems because I took too long to get to the doctor and picked the wrong insurance company.

* * *

Three days after speaking with Andrea from WAHA, Ken and I were scheduled to meet again with Leanne, the nurse we had met briefly the week before, during the chemo training session with Kateri. We had discussed the possibility of joining the clinical trial she was locally managing.

I wanted some good to come out of the agony I was about to go through with chemotherapy and its reported side effects. Maybe this trial would find another breakthrough like Herceptin; I had seen part of a Lifetime movie the previous year about the man who developed Herceptin and got FDA-approval via a clinical trial. Of course, I did not know at the time that this wonder drug would be needed by me a year later because of my aggressive HER2/neu cancer.

Maybe other women would be spared going through what I was going through at the moment. Husbands, too.

Speaking of husbands, mine dropped me off at the east tower of the hospital and went to park the car. In a rush, I walked into the window. It said east tower, dang it, so I knew I was in the right spot. Oh, I have to go around the corner and walk through the door, not the plate glass window.

Leanne, the clinical trial nurse, was inside waiting for us.

"Maria, nice to see you again." She didn't mention my run-in with the front window, which she must have seen. "Is Ken not coming?"

"He's parking the car."

The first thing Leanne said to Ken when he came in and sat down was, "You look just like Jim Carrey."

"What?" he asked in shock.

"Hasn't anyone ever told you that before?"

"Never."

"Don't you think he looks like Jim Carrey?" she asked me.

"Not really. He better be funny, though, in the next couple of weeks. I'm going to need all the humor I can get."

Ken took his Jim Carrey butt over to the restrooms and Leanne and I took a few minutes to get to know each other a bit better. I told her that the kids and I were trying to get our small flower stand open. "Yeah, it's called Wayside Wisteria and I started it to show them how to run a business. The first order of business would probably be to actually be *open* for business."

"That sounds like a good idea."

"I have no illusions that we'll become millionaires from the venture, but it's fun. Piano lessons pay the bills. Well, Ken pays the bills, but you know what I mean."

"You're very creative, aren't you?" she asked me, her soothing voice calming my frayed nerves.

"Yes, I guess I am."

Ken came back and sat next to me on the couch in the waiting room. Leanne was on the other side of me, and began explaining a few more details of the clinical research program that we needed to finalize before the EKG that would be happening in half an hour.

Ken held up a brochure titled "Free Women's Health Screening." "I'm sorry, Leanne," he said, "but I need to interrupt while I'm thinking about it."

"That's okay, Ken, what is it?"

"I'm supposed to be calling some girl named Meredith," he pointed to the inside of the glossy advertisement, "but I don't remember why. Did I get this from you?"

Leanne, continuing in her patient, soft manner, replied, "Is that maybe from HAMMA?"

Ken looked at her, confused. A small light came into his eyes and he said, "Oh, you mean WAMMA?" Now Leanne was confused, but it didn't matter because we all started giggling.

"Hamma, wamma, bing bang." Ken said what we were all thinking. Of course, he really meant WAHA, but the word WAMMA was what came out.

"How does that song go again?" I asked. "Ooh, ah, ooh, ah, ah, something-something, walla walla bing bang..."

When we were done singing and discussing the clinical trial, Ken and I went to the fourth floor for my EKG. I couldn't believe how fast this heart test was compared to the echo Brooke had performed on me five days earlier.

"Hey, Mom, how did it go today?" Adriana asked when Ken and I got home. She was scrapbooking at one end of the dining room table while Jonathan and Michael sat at the other end playing Monopoly together.

"Oh, Adriana, I'm so sick and tired of doctors already." I stood behind her and smoothed her long blond hair back from her forehead so I could see her green eyes look up at me. "Can you stop scrapbooking for a little bit? You and me need to get to Costco for a few groceries because I start chemo on Wednesday. I need to be prepared."

"Well, I'm going back to the office," Ken interjected. "Mer, if you need anything, make sure you call my cell phone. Jonathan and Michael, I want you two doing some yard work while I'm at work and Mom and Adriana are at the store," Ken said over his shoulder as he walked out the back door.

Adriana and I were standing in line at Costco to pay when Adriana's cell phone rang. People have long ago given up trying to call mine since I ignore it on a regular basis. Adriana handed the phone to me in annoyance.

It was Ken. "Mer, Leanne made a mistake this morning and forgot that we needed to have an MRI done right away. Today."

"I've already had an MRI done," I said, cupping my hand over the phone. I'm sure the Costco cashier didn't want to hear about my medical problems.

"I know, but—"

I stopped him. "I'll call you back in five minutes. Can't talk right now." I'm a great multitasker for a lot of things, but talking on the cell phone always flusters me.

"Call me back in *less* than five minutes. We have to be there right away."

So much for lunch. I'd somehow missed that detail. I felt my blood sugar dropping by the minute and the headache coming on. I paid for the groceries and followed Adriana to the car. She put the items we had purchased into the back seat while I called Ken back to calm him down.

"We need to go to Bellingham right away," he said in a panic.

"Ken, listen. I've already had an MRI. I'm sure there's some sort of simple mistake." I didn't want to do another one of those tests. They took forever and cost over $5,000 apiece.

"It's a prerequisite for the clinical trial. The MRI needs to be done within the past four weeks."

"It *has* only been four weeks, hasn't it?" I asked in amazement. My, how time flies when you're having cancer.

"No, the test was done on April 23."

"That was only four weeks ago." My blood sugar plummeted a few more degrees.

"You're skipping May," Ken realized.

What? What would happen once I started chemotherapy and got the chemo brain that Kateri talked about?

At home, all three kids started putting the groceries away while I stumbled in search of food. Ken would be here soon to pick me up.

Instead of eating lunch, I got sidetracked trying to help out. The milk was quickly put away, my water bottle was filled up with ice cubes again—at least I'd get some water.

"Guess what, Mommy?" Jonathan beamed. "I straightened out all the pots for Wayside Wisteria."

"That's great, Jonathan," I praised him.

Michael ran out the door with the chicken and meatballs to put them in the freezer, so all I saw was the back of his blond head. Ken arrived home from the office and we hopped back in the car and headed out of the driveway.

"What time do we have to be there?" I asked him.

"Four o'clock."

The clock on the dashboard said 3:38 and I stated the obvious. “We’re going to be late.”

“I know, but the girl knows we’re coming. Everything will be fine.”

I was so hungry.

By the time I made it to the dressing room, changed into the gown, and sat across from the woman who was going to help me, my headache was good and strong.

“Hi, I’m Bree. Have you had an MRI before?” she said, spouting her regular line.

“Yeah, six weeks ago on 4/23. I think you helped me.” Two stinkin’ weeks over the deadline. Maybe this clinical trial wasn’t such a good idea after all.

Bree really looked at me. “I think you’re right.”

I had forgotten how loud the knocking of the MRI machine was. Extra loud when you had a pounding headache going on.

Denise, another nurse, took the IV out of my arm and told me it was her birthday.

“Hey, you should go to Anthony’s.” I glanced down at my watch. “They have this great Sunset Dinner from four o’clock to six o’clock. It’s way cheaper.”

“Maybe I’ll go there.”

Maybe I will, too. Ken and I can go there and pretend we still have a social life.

She herded me out of the room. “Turn left. Your clothes are right down there. And, thanks for the info on Anthony’s.”

I started to turn right.

“Maria, it’s the other way.”

“Are you sure?” I asked. “I’m so disoriented. Hunger, I

guess." I walked to the end of the hallway and turned around to yell, "I'm not normally this stupid."

She probably thought, "I'll bet."

We bypassed Anthony's and ended up with toast for dinner when we got back home. I landed on the couch, next to Adriana, who sat reading her book. I seemed to be doing that more and more. Before I got cancer, I had boundless energy and only occasionally became fatigued when my thyroid medication was off. Now, I was becoming a permanent fixture on the couch, in between running from one doctor appointment to the next, of course.

Adriana put her book down. I turned on the television. The second the volume blasted, Michael and Jonathan appeared out of nowhere. If I had yelled for them to dust some furniture for me or vacuum something, I would never have found them.

Ken was the last to join the group. He had just filed away the paperwork generated from today in the Cancer Box.

The movie *My Girl* with Jamie Lee Curtis came on.

"Isn't there anything else on?" Michael complained.

"This is a great movie, Michael. You'll love it," I answered. "Besides, I have the remote. I haven't seen this for a long time, but I remember I liked it."

About halfway through the movie, the little girl on the screen began to sing, "Ooo eee,ooo ah ah, ting tang, Walla walla, bing bang, Ooo eee ooo ah ah, ting tang, Walla walla bing bang" with her best friend, played by Macaulay Culkin—the same song Ken, Leanne, and I had sung just that morning.

God sure has a sense of humor.

Who can be sad and think about bean-counting and death when they have that happy song running through their head?

Chapter Nine
Appointment With the Devil

Adriana sat in the driver's seat, Jonathan occupied the back seat, reading his Zits comic book—for once, he was quiet—and me? I sat clutching the passenger door handle. I was not looking forward to this at all.

"Mom, I thought chemo was supposed to be on Wednesdays," Adriana said.

"It was supposed to be, but Dr. Hoffman let me switch to Thursdays. I'm going to start going to that writing class every Wednesday. You should come with me sometime." Adriana was a great writer herself and I wanted to encourage her.

"Are we still stopping by Ross?" she asked. Adriana was also a great shopper.

"Yep. I need to return that red coat. For once, something's way too big. Think I'll dance all the way to the customer service counter to return it." I checked to be sure I had the Emla. It was right there in the Cancer Box by my feet, along with the plastic wrap that Dr. Williamson had told me to put over the medicine.

"Do we have time to do any shopping before your appointment?" Adriana asked. I don't know where she got her shopping gene. Definitely not from me. One thing was for sure: I hoped she didn't get my breast cancer gene.

According to the clock on the dashboard, we still had an hour and a half before we had to be at the infusion center to meet Tami. Ken and I had been late for our chemo training session with Kateri and I was determined not to make that mistake again.

In Ross, Adriana took off for the dressing room with the tank tops she found instantly. You can do that when you're skinny as a rail. Jonathan flitted in and out between the aisles, coming back every few minutes to say hello to me. I returned my coat.

After wandering around the store aimlessly, I glanced up at the clock hanging on the wall at the front of the store. It was 1:25. My chemo was supposed to be administered at 2:30. Dr. Williamson said it would take an hour for the pain medicine to take effect.

I tracked down Jonathan, which was easy since he was so tall. "Jonathan, my medicine is out in the car, probably melting. I need to get the car keys from Adriana. Stay here and guard the rest of her stuff in the cart, okay? I'll be right back."

I made my way to the back of the store.

"Excuse me," I said to the dressing room attendant, "can I go back there and get the car keys from my daughter? I have to get my medicine right away," I babbled as if she cared. "You don't understand. I have to get chemo at 2:30 and this medicine has to be on by 1:30 for it to become effective."

Control your tongue.

"Go ahead."

"Adriana," I hissed. "Adriana, where are you?" I finally found her in the corner and grabbed the keys.

In the Toyota, I found the Emla cream right away, along with the Saran Wrap.

1:35 p.m.

I leaned forward in the front seat, Emla in my hand. How the heck was I going to get this medicine on without getting arrested for indecent exposure? The Ross parking lot was very busy. And public. I couldn't just bare my boob, where the portacath was located. Well, I could, but a policeman could also slap handcuffs on me right quick.

I tried to apply the cream, but was too self-conscious, gave up, and trudged back to the store. I high-tailed it to the bathroom. My nerves were shot.

I was in the middle of washing my hands when a loud rap came at the door. "I'll be a minute," I yelled. I blopped a dollop of the medicine on my finger and rubbed it over the top portion of my half-exposed breast. Another knock came on the door. "I'll be a minute!" I snapped. Good grief. I was going as fast as I could.

I grabbed the Saran wrap and a huge piece came effortlessly out of the box. Usually, I fought with the sticky plastic to get a few inches off the roll. This time, a large enough piece to cover three breasts came off. I slapped it on my chest and walked out of the bathroom in a huff, glaring at the woman standing there. Plastic wrap stuck out the opening of my shirt. I'm sure she thought I was nuts, but I thought she was rude.

I rounded up the kids, paid for our stuff, trying to hide the Saran Wrap, and somehow made it out of the store.

We finally made it to the infusion center.

Jonathan and Adriana went flying out of the Honda and hugged "Aunt Tami" who was just exiting her car.

"Maria, how's it going?" she asked me, over Adriana's shoulder. "Are you ready for this?"

"No." I pointed to the plastic sticking out of my shirt. "Don't even ask."

I planned on having Tami sit with me through the first infusion because I figured Adriana and Jonathan would be too nervous around needles and other sick people. I turned to them. "Adriana and Jonathan? Thanks for bringing me up here. You guys go straight home now. Clean something." I knew they would turn the television on the minute they got home, but I pretended to trust them.

When Tami and I got inside, the chemo nurse reminded me, "We'll be giving you a combination of Adriamycin and Cytoxan every three weeks. The Adriamycin, by the way, is nicknamed the Red Devil."

Within days, I understood loud and clear why it's referred to as the Red Devil. It's red when it goes in, red when it comes out—for the first one or two days after it's administered anyway—and truly is the devil. I could not stop puking.

While I was pregnant with Adriana, I had such violent morning sickness, I vomited for three months straight—losing 25 pounds in the process—and finally had to be hospitalized so that the doctors could get the resultant dehydration under control. I swore I'd never get that sick again.

Here I was, back in the same boat, minus a cute little baby. Sure, Adriamycin was supposed to save my life, but I wasn't convinced that was the case or that I even cared anymore. The nausea would not abate.

Five days into the treatment, I woke up out of a dead sleep at 2:45 in the middle of the night. I bolted straight up in bed and was surprised to learn that I had slept through the "whole night." Only, the night wasn't over, not by a long shot.

My stomach felt like it was stuck in a vise. I barely made it to the bathroom. As I sat on the toilet wondering why in the world I had chosen to drink not one, but *two* cups of Smooth Move tea the day before, I moaned in agony.

Maybe I should explain.

I haven't had constipation since I was a kid. I pride myself on being able to go to the bathroom faithfully and without too much ado. Today, however, was a different story. I felt like I was going to die. For that matter, I wished I would die so that the pain would go away.

Kateri must have warned me during the training about constipation being a side effect of this particular chemo regimen. I must have tuned her out. I didn't want the power of suggestion to cause all these horrible things to happen to my body without my consent.

I sat and tried to think of the last time that I had actually had a bowel movement. *Let's see... chemo was on Thursday, but not until the afternoon. I must have gone that morning. Thursday to Friday, Friday to Saturday, then there was Sunday, Monday, Tuesday.* Yikes. Was it really five whole days? No wonder I felt the way I did.

I wracked my brain trying to think of why this had happened to me. Didn't I have enough stress in my life lately? Going poop was one thing I could count on. It was a reliable, practical thing in my life. Maybe I got too much joy out of it, having had such a hard time when I was a kid, but come on.

As I sat there on the toilet contemplating the state of my bowels and mental status since this nightmare had begun, I realized that I had also not written anything on the new book. I was tired, sick of feeling nauseated, and not finding a whole lot to laugh about. A funny book about cancer? What could I possibly have been thinking?

"Write about the Smooth Move tea," a small voice interrupted my concentration. *Shut up*, I told the voice. *I'm busy here, if you don't mind.*

A few more moments passed. Oh boy, why did I let it get this bad? Leanne, the clinical trial nurse, efficient woman that she is, had warned me about trying to be Wonder Woman and not asking for help. I went and got the tea like she told me to. The mistake had been in taking two cups in one eight-hour period.

"Smooth Move? This is more like torment in a teabag," the voice continued.

I said, be quiet! I don't think this is very funny. That stupid cancer book can go rot. I don't want to write any more funny stories. It's just not funny to feel terrible all day long and then not be able to poop like a normal person. I don't want to write about this subject anyway. It's a private matter and should not be shared with the world.

I went back to bed, unsuccessful in my endeavor, and hoped I could fall asleep to let the tea do its work. Several hours later, I looked back at the first horrendous stomach ache as a walk in the park.

Back in my vitamin-selling days, I used to promote a similar tea and remember one customer in particular. After explicit instructions *not* to take more than half a cup the first time around, I got a phone call a day or two later after the woman had obviously taken all my smart advice and thrown it right out the window.

She coughed. "Ahem. I was just wondering... is that tea supposed to give you diarrhea?"

"Millie, please tell me you didn't."

"Didn't what?" she asked meekly.

"Take more than half a cup."

"Oh."

"Millie. I told you several times, you cannot take more than half a cup to start out because everyone reacts differently to it and it's better to be safe than sorry. You want to clean out your colon, but not in one sitting."

"Oh."

"How many did you take, Millie?"

"Two."

I groaned. Yep. She had been in agony all right.

After I hung up, hoping that she really understood how to take the tea properly, I thought, *How could she have been so irresponsible? I warned her and warned her only to take a little bit. She must have been desperate or something.* I didn't want to ask her too many pointed questions while I had her on the phone. She had had punishment enough.

Now, here I was, having my own punishment, possibly for making fun of her all those years ago. God wanted me to eat my words. Or drink them in the form of a cup of tea.

I will spare my readers the minute details. Suffice it to say that it was a long and painful night and I don't recommend taking more than one cup of Smooth Move tea at a time. In fact, like I told Millie all those years ago, I'd start with half a cup and take it at the first possible sign of a problem.

In the morning, a little groggy and disoriented, I reached over to pick up the ringing telephone. It was Tami.

"Guess what, Vern? I finally went poop after five days."

Seriously, these were the first words out of my mouth. Oh my, what had happened to me?

I could hear Tami cackling in the background.

"Vern, it's not funny. It was not a pretty sight."

"I know, but that's good, right?"

"Well, I could think of a lot of less painful things to go through. A root canal, perhaps? Being struck by lightning?"

"Well, Maria, I'm glad that things are finally working again."

"You should have seen me. At three in the morning, I'm arguing with myself about this book I'm supposedly writing."

"Aren't you glad you can focus on that instead of all this

other stuff going on?"

"All I can say, Vern, is it's a good thing that this chapter won't be in the book, eh? Some things are just better left unwritten."

Oops.

Chapter Ten
The Blogosphere and Beyond

Jonathan and I sat in Dr. Hoffman's office. "How are you doing, Maria?" he asked.

"Nausea sucks."

"You still have it? Even with the Emend?" One would think that a medicine costing $100 per pill would eliminate nausea altogether. I always was sensitive to medications.

"Yes. It definitely gets better around Day 11. Yes, I'm obsessed with counting my days now." Jonathan sat reading *Sideways Stories From Wayside School* in the chair next to me.

Dr. Hoffman consulted his notes. "It says here that I have to check your lymph nodes."

I glanced at Jonathan. He gulped and pretended to

be reading his book. He didn't know a lymph node from a freckle, so I'm sure he was worried his mother would suddenly be taking her shirt off in front of him.

I lay down on the examining table and Dr. Hoffman reached by my right armpit to examine it. He thought the lymph nodes might be a hair smaller than the last time he had checked them.

How in the world would he remember how big my lymph nodes were last time? Surely, he can't remember that. Maybe he was just trying to make me feel better. It had been a terrible week.

Dr. Hoffman went to wash his hands at the sink.

"Dr. Hoffman? I know Dr. Williamson told me that all my hair would fall out. What do you think? My hair still seems so thick." Maybe I should have left Dr. Williamson out of it. Here I was calling him a liar behind his back.

Dr. Hoffman came and helped me to a sitting position. "Well, Maria, in my ten years of practice and observing the thousands of woman who have gone through the type of chemo you are going through right now, there was only *one* woman who did not lose all of her hair."

"One woman in thousands. Wow. So, you're saying there's hope then."

When Jonathan and I returned home, I took out my laptop to type in the "one woman in thousands" comment of Dr. Hoffman's. My cancer journal had slowly evolved into material for a book. It had happened so slowly that I barely noticed the subtle change.

In February, before this cancer nightmare had begun, I had contemplated getting a website to begin my quest of becoming a published author. I contacted a friend of mine. "Hi, Laurie?"

"Hey, Maria, how are you doing?"

"I'm great." One short month later, that would all change, but for now, I was oblivious to my upcoming diagnosis. "I'm just about done with that novel I was telling you about. I thought that in the meantime, I would get a website up and running. Are you interested in doing that for me?"

"Sure."

Laurie had several kids, but she was a whiz with computers, and the one I wanted to be my webmaster.

I explained what I wanted the website to look like. "I'll get back to you with the rest of the information as soon as I get it all together, Laurie, but you can start with that, right? Keep track of your time so I know what to pay you."

What I didn't know at the time was that it would take me four months to get back to her, what with the mammogram, ultrasounds, biopsies, MRIs, and countless doctor appointments to get through.

Our second conversation, those four months later, went a lot differently.

"Hello, Laurie?"

"Maria, I'm so sorry to hear about your cancer diagnosis. How are you feeling?"

"Tired, tired, tired. Nauseated."

She laughed, a little hesitantly.

"Do you still want to be my webmaster?" I asked.

"Of course." She sounded surprised that I was still planning to go through with the website.

"I still want to have a home page and a biography page. I never did give you the actual information, did I?"

"No. You were going to get back to me." She paused. "It's totally understandable that you didn't, of course."

After I explained a few items I wanted included on the home page, I explained the main reason that I wanted to get the site up and running: "The last item will be a blog. I've been going to that writing class in Coupeville every week and I listened to a great speaker talk all about blogs. Most of it was way over my head—gidgets, podcasts, and search engines. I'm sure you know what all those things are. What I mainly want to do is write a post every couple days; my email inbox is hopelessly flooded with well-wishing people wanting to know what's going on with me and I can't keep up."

"It's really easy to set up a blog."

"That's why you're my webmaster." A huge load had been taken off my shoulders.

Laurie had that website up and running within a week and I was very proud of it.

It only took about *two* weeks for the Red Devil poison to start curdling my hair follicles. My hair began to fall out in clumps.

I called Adriana, Michael, and Jonathan into the laundry room and put the haircutting cape around my neck. Ken took out the Wahl kit I had purchased several years before to cut the hair of everyone in the family. Now, it was my turn.

"Why are you cutting it, Mom?" Michael asked. "Don't you want to wait until it falls out on its own?"

"And have to vacuum up hair every day? No thanks. Adriana, grab my left hand, Michael my right," I commanded.

"Jonathan... um... I guess you get my feet." I wanted to make sure they all felt included in this momentous occasion of my becoming bald.

Ken took the scissors and began cutting. I alternated between laughing hysterically, crying, and being very ticklish. Adriana let go of my left hand and switched places with Ken. It was her turn to trim some hair.

"How you doing, Mer?" Ken asked.

"I'm fine. It's just hair." I tried to sound chipper about having my head shaved, but I wasn't quite achieving it. Would Ken wake up in the middle of the night and start screaming in terror before he realized it was me next to him? I didn't want to give my husband a heart attack.

Michael and Jonathan were next; I think they enjoyed it a little too much. I had given them countless haircuts, and they complained every single time. I told them they could go to the nearest hairdresser anytime and be sure to bring their wallets with them with at least a ten dollar bill inside.

After posting the hair incident on the blog Laurie had set up for me, I made a silent little promise to myself that I would not blog anything embarrassing about myself. The next thing I knew, I recounted the following story:

> I don't know what's with the delayed reaction of the water retention pill I took yesterday morning, but it decided to kick in today on the hour-and-a-half drive to Freeland for my all-day writing class. I wasn't early, by any means, which didn't help the situation.
>
> I was only halfway there when it hit me. I began to break out in a cold sweat. I kept

thinking, "Where are all the gas stations and stores?" Normally, I liked the fact that they were few and far between and I could enjoy the ocean view and tall cedars.

I was wearing a new skirt and I looked pretty good. I considered pulling over to the side of the road. I wondered if I would be able to... first of all, not get arrested... second of all, pee without getting it all over my skirt.

The sign said *Freeland... 17 miles* when I was getting close to going off the deep end. Seventeen miles takes *forever* when your bladder cannot contain another drop.

I reminisced about joking with one of the chemo nurses (when she explained the possibility of diarrhea as a side effect) that I should get some Depends diapers just in case. I really wished I had one now. It didn't matter that I was driving 55 miles per hour; I would find a way to get that diaper on.

When I got to the class, the teacher greeted me warmly. I threw my purse, 88,000-word manuscript, laptop, and notes for the cancer book down on the table and yelled, "Where's the bathroom?!" Of course, it was being used. Would the agony never end?

I may just go buy some Depends diapers yet.

Oh my goodness, what had happened to me? Here I was blabbing about my bodily functions on the World Wide Web.

The next day, Ken and I were ushered into Dr. Hoffman's office. We were a bit early, so I took out my laptop to work on my book. I sped past the "I've Misplaced My Underwear... Or Was It My Brain?" chapter and was halfway through the "Tender Mercies and Timely Blessings" chapter when the doctor walked into the room.

Flustered, I tried to hit the save button, but pressed the "save as" button instead and almost dropped my laptop in the process. Dr. Hoffman saw my predicament and saved the day by catching the computer on the way down.

"Thanks, Dr. Hoffman," I said, cheerfully.

"No problem," he replied. "Did you just have a hard drive failure and lose everything?"

"No, I think I actually doubled the size of my document and now have two."

He must not have understood me, because he asked, "You playing games?"

Ken cut in, "She's working on her book."

"About this experience?"

I nodded, getting ready to apologize for what I was doing.

He immediately rolled with the punches and got into it. "Well, I better make sure that I see a copy of the book first. The treatment better go well, or she'll write, 'That bastard!' I better watch myself."

I piped up, "I would never say that about you. I like you. However, that insurance company—the one I won't be able to mention by name—*they're* the bastards."

"You mean the company that starts with Crappy and ends with Insurance Company?"

"That would be the one," I responded.

"So, I want to know who's going to play me."

"Pardon me?"

"Liam Neeson or Danny DeVito, what do you think?"

"Oh." He wanted the non-existent book turned into a movie already.

"Well, Liam Neeson and Danny DeVito would each put a different slant on things, wouldn't they?" Dr. Hoffman continued.

It was strange. Of the two oncologists I was seeing, I had somehow pictured Dr. Hoffman as thinking I was a bit nuts and would try to shut me down if I brought up the book in his office. I figured Dr. Williamson would not only show interest in the book, but he would be open to endorsing the book for me someday since he, himself, had been on ABC News and 20/20.

"Maria's been feeling really sick from this Red Devil chemo," Ken relayed.

"I do feel like horse-puckey," I offered. "I'm trying to keep my positive attitude."

"I see that. I think it's great that you're writing a book about it. You'll be able to reach out and help others."

I don't know how helpful I was to Jonathan several weeks later.

It had been eight days since the third Adriamycin/ Cytoxan treatment and all the little tricks I implemented to avoid throwing up—sucking on Mentos, taking anti-nausea medication, pretending to be in a hot tub—just weren't enough. I had a hard time keeping my food down.

There was no one home—not that the family could have done anything for me, except possibly scrape me off the bathroom floor and drag me back to bed. I finally managed to fall asleep for an hour until the phone rang, waking me up. It was Jonathan.

"Mom, I'm at Value Village with Adriana and there's this really cool oil painting here and it's of the ocean and seagulls and a lighthouse and you know how we're decorating my room in that kind of stuff and it's only $9.99 and it has a really nice frame and it matches my room and I could take a picture of it with the cell phone and send it to you and I can use my own money and everything and can I get it please, please, please?"

What I felt like saying was, "Jonathan, you could steal that painting and do crystal meth right now for all I care because I feel like death warmed over." Of course, I didn't want him to steal or succumb to drugs at the age of thirteen or any other age for that matter, but it sure was hard to concentrate when I was trying to hang onto my marbles and my stomach all at the same time.

I considered hiring a nanny to ensure the kids didn't fall into ruin during this whole cancer business, but for now, I waited for Jonathan and Adriana to come home, so that I could sit on his bedroom floor, gaze at his new painting, and dream of the ocean and the Caribbean.

Chapter Eleven
Second, Third, and Fourth Opinions

They say that cancer patients should get a second opinion.

I received a total of five opinions from both sides of the fence, medical and naturopathic. Every single one of the doctors Ken and I consulted agreed: "If you want to save your life, you need to do chemotherapy."

I thought if I kept searching, I'd find a doctor who would tell me what I wanted to hear. "Well, Maria, in my professional opinion, I would go to the Bahamas, hit every hot tub and beach you can find, take obscene amounts of vitamins and freshly squeezed fruit and vegetable juices, and let the cancer float away on a big cloud of denial."

Second and third opinions don't always come from

doctors. One day, I was walking through Fred Meyer, shopping for green onions, when I saw an old friend of mine. I was in a big hurry and if I didn't get moving, I wouldn't be prepared for my weekly writing class, the one pleasant constant in my life.

"Hi, Marie, how are you?"

I could tell by the tone of her voice that she had heard about my cancer. "Other than the nausea, joint pain, depression, and diarrhea, I'm fine."

"I've been wondering how you are. I ask Julie once in a while how you're doing."

"I'm plugging along." I put the green onions back down and got a cucumber instead. Onions would probably be too strong for my stomach and new digestive problems.

"You haven't had your mastectomy yet?"

"No." I didn't want to be reminded of the surgery slated for January. The whole idea sent shivers up my spine.

"Well, I don't understand why those doctors are taking so long. If it were me, I'd just have them lop off *both* those things right away so I didn't have to worry about it."

Things? Those were my breasts she was referring to.

"Yeah, Marie, I'd have them fix it so my boobs weren't sagging down to my belly button."

I stared at her and thought, *That might be your problem, lady, but for now, my boobs are still where I want them to be. Connected to my body and still a bit perky for their age, if I do say so myself.*

"Yep, that's what I'd do, the whole nine yards."

I felt like screaming at her that she should go right ahead and do that, then. Instead, I started explaining. "Well, the doctors have all agreed that the damage has probably already been done and they need to kill the cancer before it multiplies and spreads to other parts of my body." Why did I feel this incessant need to explain myself to people all the time, especially people who didn't have my best interest at heart?

I had four more months to enjoy my right breast, damaged as it was. I'm sure Ken wanted to enjoy it also. We had decided together that we did not plan on removing it prematurely.

One morning, I was once again lying on the couch trying to keep my nausea at bay. I sat up. "Ken?"

He rushed to my side. "What is it? Are you going to throw up? You want a bucket?"

I practically twisted the collar off his shirt and put my nose close to his face. "I… must have… Bit-O-Honey."

"Huh?"

"Bit-O-Honey. I must have some right this minute."

"That's candy, isn't it? Remember what Dr. Burton said about all that sugar."

"I don't care. I need some. WD Foods should have some."

Ken grabbed his wallet and went flying out the door. I stayed on the couch, trying to sip my lemony ice water and suck on Mentos. I was so sick of both.

The phone rang about twenty minutes later.

"I'm at Fred Meyer. I can't find the Bit-O-Honey."

"Fred Meyer doesn't carry Bit-O-Honey." Where has he been? Everyone knows that Fred Meyer doesn't carry that candy. I knew I was getting snippy, but I didn't care. "I told you to go to WD Foods. What are you doing at Fred Meyer?"

“Is there anything else you need?” he asked patiently and quietly. I didn’t know how he put up with me sometimes.

“Wheat Thins.” Don’t ask me why they popped into my brain all of a sudden.

“I’ll get some then.”

“Don’t forget the Bit-O-Honey.”

“I won’t.”

A few hours later, Ken walked into the living room. “I’m going to Anacortes to pick up some firewood,” he told me.

“That’s kind of far away, isn’t it? And how are you going to carry it?”

“In the Honda.”

“Won’t that break it?” I guess I had nothing better to do than give him the third degree. Then, it dawned on me. “Oh, you’re going to the beer-making store.”

“Yes,” he said, humbly. “Do you want to come with me?”

A two-hour round trip with lots of curvy roads? I didn’t think so, especially when I had to drive past Anacortes tomorrow for my writing class. I had to pick my battles. “No, I’m staying parked right here on this couch.”

“Are you sure?”

“Yes. Oh, wait—Haribo licorice.” I knew that the gourmet candy store right across the street from the beer-making store carried them. Ken would be right there.

“You want me to pick some up?”

“Pleeeaaase?”

I fell asleep on the couch dreaming of that licorice. Maybe it would get rid of the nausea longer than the Bit-O-Honey and the Wheat Thins had.

When I woke up, Ken still wasn’t home. I immediately

thought of the delicious black licorice that was coming... not too sweet. It brought back good memories of my days working at the cheese company where I used to sell it.

The door slammed. Oh good, there was Ken. I could hardly wait. Soon, the licorice would be in my hot little hands. I could taste it already.

Ken put his bag of supplies down on the kitchen table and went to change his clothes.

When he came back into the room, I asked him. "So, where's the Haribo licorice?"

"Shoot! I forgot it."

"Good one. Where is it?"

"Really, I forgot it."

"It's not funny. Don't mess with a nauseated woman. Where did you hide it?"

"Mer, I really did forget it."

I couldn't get mad. He had been all over town several times during this round of chemo, shopping for all kinds of different things. If it had been the other way around, I probably would have just made him eat whatever was in the house.

The next thing I knew, he was calling every store in town and looking up Haribo licorice on the Internet while I barked out suggestions. "Try Haggens. I bet they have it. I think I've seen it there."

"Look," he responded, pointing to the computer screen, "the Candy Warehouse sells five pounds of it for twenty bucks."

"That's a great deal, but I need it now."

He sat on hold again. Four stores later, he determined

that there was no Haribo licorice to be found. “Sorry, Mer, I just can’t find it.” He stood and grabbed his keys and wallet off the counter. “I need to go to the bank.”

“I’ll come,” I said, eagerly.

“Are you sure?”

“I’ve been cooped up in this house for days and Haggen’s is right across from the bank. I *know* they have that licorice there.”

“I just called there and they said they didn’t.”

“What does that employee know? He probably never even looked.”

We were halfway down the candy aisle when I saw it. I jumped up and down like a 3-year-old seeing Ronald McDonald for the first time. “I knew they had it.” I grabbed three bags of it.

The candy made me happy, but the chemotherapy was making me crabby. One day, I was talking to Rich and said something about wanting to quit chemotherapy because I was tired of how it made me feel.

Rich told me, “Maria, if you quit chemo, I’m going to kick your ass.”

I knew that he was really saying that he loved me and his life was better with me in it, but I felt like screaming at him, “You’d have to catch me first! Will you be able to do that with your smoke-filled lungs?”

Later that same week, at church a woman came up to me and raved, “You look wonderful in those scarves, Maria.”

“Thanks, Jeanette. I decided not to wear wigs, even though the hospital offered me a free one. I don’t want people to look at me and wonder if I’m having a bad hair day or if this is my real hair. This way—with the scarves—people just know I have cancer and don't surmise anything."

"Well, I have to say, last week you looked radiant. I was a bit envious of you."

Envious of me? Was she nuts? I didn't even know what to say, so I said nothing.

"Yeah, I was envious because you looked so elegant. I felt frumpy."

I almost said, "Okay, shave your head, spend lots of money on different-colored scarves, and go to it. Knock yourself out." Instead, I smiled and graciously exited the conversation.

Just in time to enter another one.

The overweight woman walked up to me and asked me how the chemotherapy was going. I don't know why she rubbed me the wrong way, but she did. Without missing a beat, I snapped back that I was going to quit it.

"Maria, you can't quit chemotherapy." She wagged her finger at me. "I'll tell you what. I'm going to sell you some vitamins that will make you feel so wonderful that you'll hop right back on the chemotherapy drugs."

Say what? First of all, lady, you could stand to lose at least a hundred pounds. Working your way toward diabetes yourself, there? I don't tell you what to eat and drink. Second of all, I sell vitamins myself and still consume them on a regular basis even though they didn't prevent me from getting Stage III cancer. Third…

Why was I getting mad at her?

I searched the crowd of congregants gathered in the narthex. Where was my little friend, Isaac? I liked his opinion. He still shared it with God daily, according to Rick and Melissa. “Heal Maria.” That was a nice opinion.

God said, “Out of the mouth of babes…”

I’m sure people meant well and there might have been validity to what they were saying, but, honestly, when I’m hanging on by a very thin thread, it is not the time to tell me how ignorant I am because I don’t feel like paying exorbitant amounts of money just to feel sick every day.

Wasn’t all of this just a crapshoot anyway? The wonder drug, the “Red Devil,” could enter my system every three weeks, shrink the tumor, damage my heart, wear down my body, make my hair fall out, and save my life. But for how long?

If the cancer metastasized, I would have gone through all the torment for nothing. It certainly didn’t seem to give me any character. I felt like a kid who doesn’t feel like going to the dentist. “I don’t want to go! Mommy, please don’t make me go to that chemo appointment again.” Hey, wait, I’m 42 years old and I can do what I want.

I hemmed and hawed about whether or not to continue my chemotherapy. No matter what I did, I felt sicker than I’d ever felt in my life.

For two days, I cried and fretted about my decision.

By Wednesday, I had to pull myself together. I was meeting Rich to pick out a bathtub. Not only is Rich great at installing walls between music rooms and laundry rooms, he is also a plumber. The only problem was, he didn’t know what he was in for at our house.

Our main bathroom has been a hazard from the beginning, since we bought our 1,900-square-foot fixer-upper out in the country. There was mold that I couldn't get rid of, no matter how much bleach I used, and rotten wood. Both of these things are not conducive to healthy living, but the true test of our patience was the *bugs*. I don't know what kind they were. The kids called them flying ants. All I knew was that bugs do not belong in a bathroom. They need to stay out in the garden and do good things like eat other bad bugs.

To complicate things further, our house was built on a slab foundation and the pipes were going to be a hassle to replace.

The alarm went off at six. My feet hit the floor, and I pulled on my underwear. They were abnormally tight. *What in the world?* Oh yeah, ever since I had made a new promise to myself to do "whatever it took to get through chemo," I discovered that Häagen-Dazs chocolate mint ice cream worked the best for nausea. I had consumed three pints over the two previous days—and while it worked wonders for the nausea, it wasn't too great for the hips, obviously. Could I really gain ten pounds that fast, or had a smaller pair of underwear sneaked into my lingerie drawer?

At the plumbing supply place, I spotted Rich's silver truck right away. He was inside the store already, looking at a jetted tub.

"Hey, Rich, how's it going?"

"I'm doing great, but I've got to tell you, you're looking a little green."

"I'm feeling real fat today on top of the nausea." I sat down in the model jetted tub and rested.

"This tub? The original price was $2,500, but I think it's on sale for 500 bucks."

My ears perked up. Who cared about tight underwear? I could take a bath every night and pretend I was in a hot tub.

"Stay right here a minute, okay?" Rich instructed.

Oh great, he was going to play the cancer card. I never used it myself. I overheard him talking to the manager. "Kids' piano teacher… Stage III… tub… sale… chemo."

Oh my goodness. I had one foot in the grave and the other on a banana peel.

I looked down at the tub again. I recalled my Aunt Ann saying that she hated her jetted tub. She could never get the mold out of the jets properly. Maybe I should rethink this. I didn't want to replace one mold problem with another.

"Maria," Rich whispered, "he's going to go check into it."

I slapped his arm playfully. "Stop using that cancer card on my account."

He grinned.

"You know, Rich, I'm thinking that I don't really need to have a tub with jets." I felt bad because he was going to bat for me, but I kept hearing Aunt Ann's voice in my head.

We wandered and discovered a standalone tub on sale. "Rich, this is the one I want. It's oversized, just like me. My hips are getting wider and wider. I thought chemo would make me lose weight, but the doctor told me most women gain at least seven pounds. I think I did that in one week already."

"You look fine."

"No, I'm serious. My underwear's really tight today." Yes, I had just told Rich about my tight underwear. He didn't seem phased by it at all. Then again, I'd heard some pretty wild things out of his own mouth. We liked to banter back and forth on a regular basis.

I quickly looked at the price tag dangling from the tub. “Regular price $1,000, on sale for $400. Let’s get it.”

“Will it fit in the bathroom, though?” he said, practical man that he was.

A light bulb went off in my head. “Hey, Rich,” I slapped him again, “you know that useless skinny closet that’s in our living room on the other side of the bathtub? Let’s rip that sucker out and re-drywall right over it. I *hate* that thing. It’s such an eyesore and not good for anything anyway.”

I’m sure Rich curses the day he met me. Every time he turned around, I had a new project lined up for him. Now, not only was he replacing the bathtub, I had him putting up new drywall.

The oversized tub was the one we purchased.

By the time I got home, I was exhausted. I wanted to drown my sorrows in some ice cream or dip in my pretend hot tub, but oops, both of them were gone.

It wasn’t until several hours later that I realized what the problem was. I hadn’t gained any weight; I had simply put my underwear on sideways. I don’t know what’s more scary: the fact that they fit sideways (sort of) or that I didn’t notice it for so long.

The other scary thing was not only were we demolishing our bathroom back to the studs and dumping items from four closets onto the floor around my piano, but Ken and the kids would soon be leaving for camp, and school started the day after they came home.

Someone shoot me.

Strangers began to come to the house. “Hi, my name

is Chris. I'm Rich's friend and I'm here to install some new wiring."

"Bernie, here. I know Rich. I'm here to install drywall where your closet used to be." It looked like Rich was using the cancer card all over town.

Then, family started to show up. My sister, Lisa, and my mom and dad stopped by. They would be installing tile in the shower and in the front foyer and helped with the prep work.

Rich's kids, Michaela and Isaac were there almost every day, helping out. Rick and Melissa came with Nathan, Alyssa, and Isaac in tow. With Adriana, Michael, and Jonathan thrown into the mix, the kid count topped out at eight.

"Hey, little Isaac," I said from my place on the couch, "come here, buddy."

He bounded over to me.

"I understand that you pray for me every day."

"Heal Maria!" he tilted his head back to demonstrate.

"You're quite the little guy, aren't you? Give me a hug."

He squeezed me tight and ran off, chanting as he went, "Heal Maria... heal Maria... heal Maria."

Keep praying, Isaac. I need all the help I can get.

After all the helpers had gone home, I was still lying on the couch, sick as a dog. Ken massaged the bottom of my feet.

"Mer, how are you feeling?" he asked as he kept rubbing.

"This remodel is going to do me in. There's dust everywhere, no shower, a bathtub in the middle of nowhere, no curtains for privacy, junk all over the floor."

"I know."

"These people are so generous helping us."

"I know that, too."

"I need to smoke that pot."

"What?"

"You heard me. I'm ready to try it. The ice cream's not cutting it anymore. This nausea sucks."

"Are you sure?"

"Yes. On one condition, though. I want the kids to be there so that there's no curiosity or sneaking around."

* * *

The whole family was seated in a circle on a blanket in the back yard.

"How do I use this... uh... is it called a bong?" I asked Ken.

"It's a pipe," he answered, tamping the marijuana into the opening.

Michael thumped his forehead with his hand. "Mom, you're so out of it."

"How do you know so much about this, anyway?" I asked.

"Oh, I smoke drugs all the time, Mom, didn't you know?" he teased.

"Hm."

"Okay, Mer," Ken interjected. "Are you paying attention?"

"I don't feel so good. I think I'm going to throw up."

"That's why we're doing this, remember? Dr. Burton said to do whatever it took to get through the chemo. We've been over this a hundred times."

"But, pot. Really?"

"Really. Okay, you have to inhale it for it to work."

I took the pipe from his proffered hand and put my lips to the opening as he lit it. I blew instead of sucking in; it went out several times.

Ken grabbed the pipe. "Oh my word. You go like this." He made it look so easy.

I tried it again. Some must have got in my system, because I began to cough. "People do this for fun? I don't think this is very fun."

"Mom," Jonathan said, "just do it. C'mon, you can do it." There was something dreadfully wrong with this picture. My son was encouraging me to smoke weed and I was obliging. The other two kids seemed to be having fun right along with him.

"Did I get any in? Do you think? Huh? Do you think I did it?" I asked Ken earnestly.

"No. You didn't." I heard the impatience in his voice.

"It made me cough."

"You're not doing it right. You do it like this." He took another deep drag.

I was getting frustrated. I never did pot as a teenager. I never drank. Well, I tried beer when I was underage, once. I thought it tasted like horse pee. How do I know what horse pee tastes like? I don't, except that's the first thing that came to my mind at the time.

Smoking? Only tried that once, too. Tami and I stole a pack of my dad's Marlboros and drove around in his Jeep and lit up a few. I didn't like it then and I didn't like it now. Smoking wasn't for me.

I took another attempt at the pot pipe in my hand.

"I think you're getting it, Mom," Adriana observed.

I felt encouraged and took another hit. Is that what it's called? What a novice I was.

I leaned into Ken. "Hey, baby, I know why you want me to smoke this pot. You just wanna get lucky tonight." A split second later, I realized what I had said and turned to look at the kids. "Oops, I'm stoned. I'm saying inappropriate things."

After the initial shock, one by one the kids fell over on the blanket, laughing. Ken and I followed. We all laughed until we cried.

Then, Ken stood up. "I'm going to weed the garden. The whole thing. And eat. Man, I'm starving. We got any snacks in the house? Cookies? Chips?"

He's stoned out of his gizzard, just for trying to show me how it's done. As for myself, I wasn't too sure I wanted to resort to marijuana again.

One thing was for sure, I was so glad when the toilet, sink, and bathtub were all hooked up in the new bathroom. I sat back in my oversized tub and let the water soak away my troubles.

"Are you sure you're okay with me going camping and leaving you home alone?" Ken asked me that night while we were in bed.

"What can you do for me? Just because I'm down and out doesn't mean you and the kids should suffer." I was trying to be valiant.

"I'm worried that you're going to need me and I'll be across the mountains."

"After this remodeling work, I think you, Rich, Rick and Melissa and all the kids deserve a break. You guys will have fun." I wasn't even jealous. I felt too tired to even think about going swimming, boating, or fishing.

"I wish I could take away all your misery, Mer."

"I know you do. Just have fun with the kids. I'll be fine."

How wrong I was. The house was empty and I stayed on the couch, hardly able to move. The nausea was so extreme. Nothing helped: not ice cream, not licorice, not Mentos, frozen blueberries, Saltine crackers, Emend from the doctor... *nothing.*

I was thankful for when I could finally fall asleep for a brief respite.

Ken and the kids would be gone for seven days. It felt like forever.

Hour after hour on that leather couch, in the silence, I thought about how awful I felt. *I no longer dread death... it would be a welcome alternative to this.*

* * *

Ken lay down on the bed next to me and put his hand on my back which was turned toward him. "The kids are in bed already. They were really tired and didn't want to disturb you since it's so late. We'll take care of all the camping stuff in the morning."

I came straight to the point. "Ken, I'm not doing chemo anymore."

He stiffened. "Mer, no."

"I can't... do... this." I sniffled. I had told myself I wasn't going to cry, but it was no use.

"You've got to keep fighting."

"I don't want to fight anymore. I'm done."

"Please," he pleaded, "don't quit." He wrapped me in his arms, which made me cry harder.

"I don't care if I live or die."

"I care if you live or die. I knew I shouldn't have left you alone," he said.

"It has nothing to do with that."

"At least promise me that you'll think about it some more." He begged me to go see Dr. Burton with him, knowing that I lean toward the naturopathic way of thinking in the whole scheme of things.

After a restless night, the next morning we sat across from Dr. Burton, whom I'd begun calling by her first name, Haley. I really liked her. She was young, wore classy clothes, and had short, curly brown hair that I admired during every appointment.

I was looking forward to being let off the hook from doing chemotherapy and beginning my carrot fast.

She asked in a firm voice, "Maria, why do you not want to continue chemotherapy? It's what we agreed on months ago, remember?"

"Well, Haley, I... uh... well..." Boy, she sure was looking me straight in the eye. I had all these reasons. Where were they all now? *Chemo is a poison, I feel horrible, I'm probably going to die anyway... Oh yeah...* "It's a crapshoot either way, so why go through this?"

"Maria, you have Stage III, locally advanced, invasive, HER2/neu breast cancer. We've talked about this."

"I know that, but... but..." I began to cry. So did Ken.

"You need to do chemotherapy. I know it's difficult and

you feel nauseated all the time, but we're going for a cure here."

What was the other option again? Oh yes, death.

"Natural medicine, Maria, is not going to work here. Sure, I can support you through the chemotherapy and minimize some of the damage that the drugs cause, but you're still Stage III. We have hope here. I don't want to have to treat you for palliative care."

I instantly thought of drool. Did I want to wear a bib and have a hospice caregiver wipe spittle from my chin? I felt like hyperventilating and throwing myself out the window. Her office was on the fourth floor after all.

The whole way home, I hardly said a word to Ken. *I know this isn't his fault, but I have no fight left in me.*

As the nausea dragged on in spite of all the tricks I tried to combat it, still the opinions kept coming. I found myself wanting to scream at overweight people, smokers, and people who drank pop or ate Fruit Loops for breakfast: "If I wanted your opinion, I would have asked for it! When you lose 100 pounds and avoid diabetes, talk to me then! When you stop chain-smoking your way to lung cancer, you can tell me what to do with *my* life!"

As I continued to deal with second, third, and fourth opinions from well-meaning friends and family telling me I had made the right decision in continuing chemo or that reconstruction of both breasts would be a great idea, it got easier to ignore them and enjoy Häagen-Dazs chocolate chip mint ice cream. My opinion of *that* is, it's mighty fine.

Chapter Twelve
My Oprah Dress

I couldn't look another chocolate chip mint pint from Häagen-Dazs in the eye.

Or Wheat Thins, Mentos, frozen blueberries, Bit-O-Honey, or Haribo licorice, for that matter. I would say that I had a sudden weight problem, but that would be lying. I'd been overweight for over 18 years now. My ideal weight at the age of 20 was 125. Two years into marriage, I had a miscarriage, my thyroid went on vacation, and consequently, my weight ballooned to 235.

I had managed to lose 25 pounds over the years, but the weight always managed to creep back up.

Already self-conscious about the extra weight that I carried around with me everywhere I went, my low self-esteem was exacerbated when Adriamycin caused my hair to fall out, the eyebrows to slip off my face, and eyelashes to leave one by one. I could hardly wait until they cut off my right breast.

Hard to feel beautiful when all of these things happen in quick succession.

Speaking of quick succession, I couldn't believe that it was already September. "Ken, I still can't believe those kids are back in school already. They say the older you get, the faster time goes."

"That's what they say."

"Well, time isn't moving fast enough, if you ask me. I wish I were all done with that wretched chemo." We were on our way home from yet another doctor's appointment.

"At least you're done with the Red Devil one. What did Dr. Hoffman say? The next treatment starts in two weeks, right?"

"Yep, September 10." It amazed me how, in spite of my chemo brain, dates still came to me easily. I was constantly counting days until my next treatment. I wanted it all to be over and get on with my life.

"What was the name of the new drug?"

"Pax-i-something, something. I think they call it Taxol. Not sure why they have to give it two names. Call it one thing and stick to it."

"What about those horse pills you have to take now?"

"Lapatinib." I separated the syllables. "That cracked me up when Leanne said, 'Don't let them touch your hands. They are chemo, after all.' That stuff's going to be floating through my system, but don't let it touch my hands?"

Ken sighed. “You’re not going to try to weasel out of this chemo, too, are you?”

“How about the next time you go through chemo, we’ll talk again.”

“That’s not fair, Mer, and you know it.”

“Well, it sure is easy for people to tell me what to do on a regular basis.” How did this turn into a fight?

“Come on, don’t lump me in with everyone. This has been hard on the whole family.”

My eyes watered. I had asked one of the nurses if that was normal and she told me that eyelashes protect your eyes. Seeing as I only have about three eyelashes left, that would explain a lot.

“Mer, did you hear what I said?”

“Yes, it’s been hard on the whole family. I didn’t mean to go out of my way to make everyone miserable.”

“That’s not what I said.”

“I’m tired. Let’s just get home. I want to get all that junk around the piano put away. It will take another three months, so I better get started.”

He ran his hands through his dark brown hair. “I can help you or maybe you could go for a walk.”

“What’s that supposed to mean?”

“Dr. Burton—I mean Haley—told you that you should exercise every day.”

“Are you saying I’m fat?” *I am fat. Tell myself I need to do something about it every other day.*

“Mer, are you just out for a fight today?”

“I’m sick and tired of feeling like this every day. I *know* I need to walk, I *know* I need to eat healthier—not that it did me any good before—but I want to crawl into bed so I don't feel the nausea." I wiped my eyes again.

We were on our road. Ken reached over and clasped my hand. "We'll get through this, okay? One day at a time."

I wiped my eyes with the other hand and pointed out, "I'm not crying."

"I know. Your eyelashes protect your eyes." He grinned. "And you don't have any."

"I'm so ugly."

"You are not."

"Ugly and fat."

"Mer."

"Okay."

What does all of this have to do with the Oprah Dress?

I bought a dress at Ross about three years ago during one of my "dropping-weight extremely-fast-due-to-my-thyroid-going-into-hyper-drive" episodes. Unfortunately, when my medication got adjusted, the weight came back on, and the dress was relegated once again to the back of the closet. I can get the dress on, but the fact that I look six months pregnant prevents me from wearing it in public.

I forgot about the dress until I took the "pitching" class; in writing lingo, that means you learn how to sell your story and yourself to an agent to get published. The teacher stood at the front of the class and instructed, "On the paper in front of you, write down your biggest goals and dreams as they relate to your writing career."

I could have written, "Get my book done before I die from cancer." Instead, I wrote down in a bold hand, *Be on Oprah.* I must confess, however, that I am *not* a public speaker. I can hardly choke out introductions at the recitals I hold for my piano students, and I mumble like a complete idiot every time.

When my original choral composition, "I Will Give You Praise," premiered at the local 2009 Tulip Festival concert, Randall, the music director, prefaced the program with a speech about how wonderful the song was and what a delight it had been to orchestrate. After my performance at the piano among the violinist, flutist, and full choir around me, I should have gracefully bowed toward the audience and waved like the seasoned performer that I am, but instead, I slithered off the stage in embarrassment.

People still tell me how much they enjoyed my creation, but all I can do is relive the humbling experience about how un-public-speaker-like I was that night.

The Oprah show? How in the world would I get through it? While I certainly wouldn't start jumping up and down on her couch, I hope I would get a huge dose of confidence and would be able to talk to her in complete, legible sentences.

"*Hello, Marie, I understand you wrote a humorous book on cancer.*"

"*Yes, Oprah. Me have stage cancer. I mean three. Stage Three. I'm a breast. Help me, help me, help me.*"

Is Oprah filmed in front of a live audience? I wonder if the producer could edit out the verbal ineptness that I would portray. While he's at it, maybe he could work a miracle and cut fifty pounds from my body.

I saved that piece of paper from the pitch class I'd taken. Then, I promptly continued resorting to sugary snacks to deal with the nausea as my weight continued to creep up. I found a kindred spirit in the most unlikely of places.

"My name is Kylie and I'll be doing your echocardiogram today."

I got undressed and Kylie began her ultrasound. She mentioned that she had not eaten breakfast and I reprimanded her and told her that was very unhealthy. Then again, I was the one lying on the table getting my heart examined.

"What about almonds?" I asked her. "You could put some of those in your pocket and snack on those."

"Well, with all the flesh-eating bacteria floating around, it's hard to eat stuff here."

Flesh-eating bacteria? Yikes.

Somehow we stumbled onto the subject of American candy versus European candy. Kylie explained how she never ate American candy when she was a kid and had continued the tradition today.

"I think American chocolate is disgusting," she said.

"I know. It's waxy and grainy," I agreed.

"I always ate Cadbury chocolate."

"Oh, have you ever had Lindt bars?" I asked her.

"Oh yeah." She adjusted the screen in front of her.

"The raspberry ones are my favorite."

"What about Kiddos?"

"What in the world are those?"

I could see her heading to some far-off place. "These shortbread biscuits drenched in this yummy, yummy chocolate."

"I'm partial to the Lu biscuits, myself. The dark chocolate ones."

"What about licorice?"

"We always had Dutch licorice at our house growing up. I used to like it but now I think it's disgusting. I think it has ammonia in it or something. I like the Haribo licorice now. It's much milder and not as sweet. I really am kind of a food snob, aren't I? I never eat Sparkle, but I adore Häagen-Dazs."

"It's like eating Twizzlers verses Red Vines. Some people like Twizzlers, but personally I think they taste like wax or plastic."

I laughed. "Do you realize we've been talking about candy for fifteen minutes?"

"We have, haven't we?"

"Probably not a good thing when you're hungry."

There was no way I was going to fit into that Oprah Dress if I indulged in eating all the junk food we had just talked about.

Chapter Thirteen
My Bucket List

Hey, what movie do you kids want to watch?" It was Labor Day and we were in the mood to hang out in front of the television. I held up three DVDs: *Sense and Sensibility*, *The Bucket List*, and *Horatio Hornblower*.

"*Sense and Sensibility*," Adriana answered.

"*Horatio Hornblower*," Jonathan answered.

"I don't care," Michael said.

Ken walked into the living room where we were all gathered. "What are we watching?" Usually, every Friday night, especially now that the kids were back in school and we were somewhat back into our regular routine, we tried to make a point of spending some time together as a family. It was nice to have an extra day, a Monday at that, to spend more time with the kids. They were growing up too fast.

"*The Bucket List*." I made an executive decision.

Four heads turned to look at me. Ah, they figured I wouldn't want to watch this particular movie because it was too close to home.

"I feel like laughing," I explained. "I also think Morgan Freeman and Jack Nicholson are good actors. You kids haven't even seen this movie yet, have you?"

"No, but I saw the scenes; isn't it about two men who are dying?" Adriana asked cautiously.

"We're all dying. Let's watch it." I walked over to the entertainment center, put *Sense and Sensibility* and the first movie of the *Horatio Hornblower* series back on the shelf, and slipped *The Bucket List* into the DVD player.

We laughed (and cried) through the whole movie.

On Wednesday, at my writing group get-together at the Coupeville Pier, I had my open laptop in front of me. I could write about how nervous I was for my first Taxol infusion the following day. *This is supposed to be a funny book.* What was funny about Taxol? I had just somehow made it through four very long months of the Adriamycin/Cytoxan chemo regimen. Mentally, I was not prepared for tomorrow.

I thought back to *The Bucket List* and Jack Nicholson and Morgan Freeman jumping out of an airplane. That's what I felt like I was doing, jumping out of an airplane, into the unknown. More chemo, more side effects. I could hardly wait.

Hey, maybe I should make my own bucket list, I thought. *I could be dying. Even if I'm not, I like to make goal lists. Heck, I don't know what else to write about, so what do I have to lose?*

I knew one thing for sure. Skydiving was not going to be on my list. I was too chicken. It was hard enough for me to get into a plane, much less to jump out of one.

Usually I know exactly what I want and go after that. Cancer has changed that in me. No matter how much I want to publish a book or see my daughter get married and have babies, I might not have that choice. I may be dead.

Rowena, to my right, was typing furiously on her historical fiction novel while Andrea looked over a manuscript to my left.

Normally, writer's block is not a problem for me. I tend to type too much and then spend the next couple of weeks editing away. I talk too much, I type too much.

"September 9, 2009," I typed into the laptop. I had this obsessive need to type in the date every time I added anything to my ongoing manuscript.

"Bucket List," I typed next. Wow. Two whole words added to the length of my book since the date wouldn't be included in the final copy. I better work a little faster than this or I really would be dead before my book had a chance of seeing the desk of a publisher.

I sighed and looked upward at the ceiling of the coffee shop where we met.

Come on, Marie, you can do this. Just type something, anything. What do you want out of life, especially now that it might be shortened?

Ding! I got it.

Now that we were remodeling our bathroom, I had a spark of hope that we could do the same to our kitchen. I've always been into cooking and baking, especially in the fall. Every year, I try to add a new recipe. It was important for me to have traditions that the kids could pass on to their kids. "Yeah, your grandmother made these Pumpkin Cream Cheese Muffins. They were to die for."

Every Christmas, I would make Creamy Dreamy Fudge and Adriana, Michael, and Jonathan began getting their friends hooked on it. Rich, Michaela, and Isaac came over one day and ate a whole log of my fudge in one sitting. It made me happy.

It was hard to create all these masterpieces in our 6-by-10 kitchen with no window. Yes, you read that correctly. Six by ten. I'm sure there are smaller kitchens around, maybe in mobile homes and RV trailers, but that's the size of the kitchen I inherited when we bought our dream property out in the country.

I stared at the laptop in front of me. "Bucket List" was all I had accomplished in the twenty minutes I had been sitting and thinking about what I wanted to write. I was too busy dreaming about pumpkin muffins and fudge.

"Number One. Get my kitchen done before I am dead." Was that being too pessimistic?

Ken and I had talked about having our kitchen remodeled so many times over the past 11 years—more earnestly when the wood around the sink was rotting and had to be replaced—but every September, we always use our remodeling money to send the kids to private school instead. I hope they're being remodeled into model students, ready to contribute to society, since we're spending a small fortune on them.

Maybe I should take out "before I am dead," even though it added four extra items to my word count.

What else? That's all you want to do in life? Have a remodeled kitchen?

"Number Two. Publish a book."

My novel, *The Lighthouse Never Dims*, still sat on my computer, fully edited. I needed to do something with it. Now, here I was working on a memoir about having cancer. Maybe this goal for my bucket list was a bit too lofty. What was I thinking? I began to backspace over Number Two on my imaginary bucket list.

Hey, Jack Nicholson and Morgan Freeman saw the Pyramids and the Taj Mahal. Granted, Jack Nicholson was a billionaire. You can do a lot of things when you're filthy stinking rich.

Wait a minute. These are fictional characters, I reminded myself.

I retyped, "Number Two. Publish a book." I was going to think positive. I had heard story after story about authors who were ready to give up, but stuck with their goals anyway. I determined to be one of those people.

Rowena seemed to be stumped in her manuscript. Ha! I was suddenly on a roll.

Number Three... Number Three... *Okay, what else do you want to do? Write a book and then have a nice cup of tea in your new kitchen to celebrate. What next?*

How many items did Jack Nicholson and Morgan Freeman have on their list, about 10? That was a nice round number to aspire to.

1. Get my dream kitchen.

2. Publish a book.

Jack and Morgan—what were they, my best friends now?—went to all these exotic places: the Taj Mahal, the Pyramids, Hong Kong, the Himalayas.

Maui. That's where I wanted to go.

Ken and I spent our honeymoon 19 years ago on Sugar Beach on the island of Maui, and while we sat in the warm sun on the soft sand all those years ago, we made a promise to each other that we would come back for our 25th anniversary.

Six more years to wait? I might be dead by then. It sure seemed a lot funnier to watch a comedy about bucket lists and dying. When it came to real life, it wasn't so funny anymore.

I started to argue with myself. Even if we did go earlier, how in the world would we pay for it? How could we justify going at all? Other people were paying for our tuition, contributing to our medical bills, and bringing us meals.

"Number Three. Go to Maui for our 20th anniversary." I wrote it down anyway. Jack and Morgan didn't think they were going to do half the things they did either. I didn't care any longer that they were fictional characters in a movie. If you write down something, it's supposed to come true. I had heard and read that countless times and I was going to believe it.

1. Get my dream kitchen.

2. Publish a book.

3. Go to Maui for our 20th anniversary.

I could shoot for losing some weight before going to Hawaii. I was already going to be self-conscious with one breast. Even if I wasn't trying to lose weight for the cause of looking awesome on the beach, I had always told myself I didn't want to die a fat woman. I wanted a skinny coffin. I'd never been so obsessed with death before, but I guess cancer makes a person a bit more paranoid about waking up the next day.

1. Get my dream kitchen.

2. Publish a book.

3. Go to Maui for our 20th anniversary.

4. Lose 25 pounds before going to Hawaii.

I scratched out the last entry and wrote, "Fit into my Oprah Dress" instead; might as well kill two birds with one stone.

What else? What did Morgan Freeman and Jack Nicholson do besides get paid millions of dollars to pretend to be two other people? They said they wanted to see something majestic. Haleakala, the "House of the Sun" crater in Maui would be majestic enough for me.

The two characters also wanted to laugh until they cried. Well, I'm writing a funny book about cancer. I guess that's as humorous as I'm going to get.

Jack Nicholson kissed the most beautiful girl in the world. I'm already married to a great guy and can kiss him any time I want.

My list is only going to have five items because I really want them to all happen and this is real life, not some screenplay written for two great actors.

1. Get my dream kitchen.

2. Publish a book.

3. Go to Maui for our 20th anniversary.

4. Fit into my Oprah Dress.

I knew what the last item would be. It was a simple thing, really. In all the years I've been married and kept my own house, I've wanted a patio, complete with a table, chairs, and an umbrella, so that we can sit outside as a family. We love to eat out of doors and there's never any place to sit.

This past summer, we tried eating on a blanket in the back yard, but I had just had the biopsy done and I could hardly get up off the ground. Even when I smoked pot, I had to sit on a blanket, although that's probably the hippie way to do it anyway.

1. Get my dream kitchen.

2. Publish a book.

3. Go to Maui for our 20th anniversary.

4. Fit into my Oprah Dress.

5. Get a patio set and concrete poured in the back yard.

It took me a full 45 minutes to come up with five items for my bucket list. Rather than be discouraged that I didn't come up with 10 things, I came to the conclusion that for the most part, I am content with my life just the way it is.

Chapter Fourteen
I Think My Liver's Mad at Me

During my first round of Taxol/Lapatinib at the infusion center, Leanne, the clinical trial nurse sat down next to me where I reclined in my green chair.

"How are you, Maria?"

"Not very excited about today, that's for sure."

"Well, I thought we could go over a few things. Would that be okay?"

"Sure." Did I have a choice? I was hooked up to an IV. It would be hard to run.

"I wanted to talk about a few of the side effects you could expect."

Erg. I was sick of side effects.

"Diarrhea is very common with Taxol and Lapatinib."

How could she have such a soothing voice and talk about something so wretched?

"Great. I can hardly wait."

Leanne then proceeded to give me not one, not two, but *five* boxes of Imodium. I've never taken Imodium in my life and didn't want to start now. "You realize, Maria, that you might not need these, but it will be nice to have them in case."

"Why don't you just give me one? Five's too many."

"Really, I think you should take five."

How much diarrhea did she think I was going to have anyway?

"Also, Lapatinib has been known to cause all-over body rashes, especially on the face."

"Why does everything have to happen to the face?" I joked. "First the eyebrows, then the eyelashes. It was hard enough to deal with being bald. It's a good thing Ken still loves me, although I'm getting uglier by the day."

"Maria, you'll get through this."

I sighed. "I know. Okay, rashes. What else?"

"Wait a minute. It's very important that you use plenty of moisturizer to help with the rashes. Don't be afraid to put tons of it on."

"Lotion. Any particular brand?"

"I have a few for you here." She handed me several bottles. Add it to the five boxes of Imodium, and pretty soon I would need a suitcase to get out of here.

"Dixie told me last week that I would probably have joint pain requiring aspirin. How common is that?"

"Well, you know, Maria, everyone is different."

"This is me we're talking about, Leanne. I get everything. I'm very sensitive to medicines." I got a shiver up my spine just remembering the Adriamycin/Cytoxan chemo that I had completed only three weeks earlier.

"You will be getting Taxol every week for three weeks and then the fourth week will be your 'free' week. Do you understand that?"

"Can't we just speed things up and get it all over with? Go every week, march straight through, and be done with it?"

"Maria, it doesn't work that way."

"Darn."

"You will take the Lapatinib every day. Five pills. And don't get them on your fingers. You have the pill organizer I gave you, right?"

I nodded.

By the time of my next Taxol infusion, one week later, I still had not opened the Imodium boxes Leanne had pressed upon me. Ken had already purchased one box of Imodium, being the good, attentive, caring husband that he is, and it resided in our medicine cabinet among the Emla cream and Eucerin lotion that I had begun slathering over my body on a regular basis.

* * *

"Hey, Debbie, you want some of my Cheerios?" I asked my driver of the day. We sat in the infusion center, waiting for the nurse to hook me up to an IV.

It was still hard for me to get used to being in one big room with so many other cancer patients. I always felt like

I was snooping into their private lives. I noticed today that the person to my left had closed the curtain in between our respective spaces.

"That's okay, Marie. I'm fine."

Debbie's daughter, Olivia, is in Adriana's grade, while her other daughter, Abigail, is one year older. They all attend Mount Vernon Christian together. The minute I met Debbie two years ago when Olivia and Adriana were freshman, I knew that we were going to become good friends. I was right. She was adorable, funny, affectionate, and sweet. We clicked right off the bat.

"So, you've never been here before, right?" I asked Debbie.

"No, but I'm so glad I came." She tucked her bobbed hair behind her left ear and fairly sparkled.

"I guess Tami or Susie usually drive me. It would be nice if you could meet them."

"I met Tami that time at your house, but I've never met Susie."

"I've known her forever and she's one of the kindest people you'll ever meet."

"Do you want anything?" Debbie asked.

"I'm fine. I've got my Cheerios."

Dana, my nurse of the day, finished drawing blood and began to label the vials. "Dana, I almost forgot." I reached into the big bag next to me I used to organize the weekly piles of stuff I dragged with me. "Leanne gave me five boxes of Imodium last week and I... don't... want... them," I said emphatically as I plunked them down on the table.

Her eyes opened wide.

"I know," I said. "I don't know what Leanne was thinking. That's a crapload of drugs, isn't it? Ha, ha, that's funny. Get it?" If she got it, she didn't think it was funny.

Debbie did, though. She burst out laughing.

The curtain next to my area swung open widely and Kateri, my chemo-trainer, stuck her head through the opening. "Keep it down over here, would you?"

"Ah, stop being so grumpy," I warned.

Debbie looked at me hesitantly.

"Oh, it's all right," I explained. "Kateri's okay. I stalk her on a regular basis."

I explained how I had forced Kateri to let me take her picture the first time we met in case I "wrote a book someday."

"By the way, Kateri," I addressed the closed curtain, "I put that picture on my website."

"What?" The curtain swayed. "You better not have. You told me you wouldn't do that without my permission."

"I know. I was just pulling your leg. Calm down, missy."

"You better watch yourself."

"The picture's on the website." The curtain parted again.

"You just said—"

"I cropped you out. It's just me. Gotcha."

"Sheesh, am I glad that you're not my patient today," Kateri said in a mock-harsh tone.

"Me, too."

Debbie asked, "Is it always like this?"

"Yep," I replied.

Dana turned to me and held up the vial she had filled. "I'll bring this to the lab and let you know what your blood counts are for today."

Sounded like fun to me. Oh, for the days when I didn't have to even be conscious that I have blood in my body.

I eyed the five boxes of Imodium Dana had left behind. "Isn't that nuts?" I asked Debbie, who nodded.

"I guess Leanne thought I'd have a lot of diarrhea. Of course, now that I'm giving them all back, I'll have the runs the second I get home."

"Murphy's Law," Debbie agreed.

"Wait. I hope I make it home first. Wonder if I should get a Depends diaper here before I leave," I fretted.

Kateri walked over. "You two better be quiet over here. You're disturbing the other patients."

"You better watch it, Kateri, or I'll stick Imodium in your drinking water," I warned. "You won't poop for a week."

* * *

Over the next few weeks, I tried to pay attention to my body and prevent as many side effects, including diarrhea, as I could. I had glutamine powder from Haley, which she said would help with neuropathy and the digestive problems the new drugs could cause.

I thought I was handling the new chemo regimen—Taxol by infusion and five Lapatinib horse pills per day—pretty well. Then again, there was only one way to go and that was up. The Red Devil pretty much brought a person down as close to the grave as you could get without actually getting *into* it.

Then, the new symptom descended.

One Saturday night, I plunked down in front of *NCIS* with the kids, proud of the two flowerbeds I'd rototilled, the five bushes I'd transplanted, and the edging I had done that day. I scratched my left ear. It itched like a son of a gun. *I must have been bitten by a bug while I was out working in the yard today.*

On the first commercial break, I ran to the new bathroom and checked it out. My ear had swollen to where it was sticking out a bit from my head.

I went back to Abby and DiNozzo and all the other interesting characters on the marine show, kept scratching my ear, and didn't think much of it until my right ear started to itch.

The next morning, Sunday, I went to the bathroom to get ready for church and noticed my face was beet red. Did the mosquitoes have a party on my face overnight? There were no bites, and it didn't itch like my ears, but it sure was red.

"What happened to your face?" Ken exclaimed when he saw me.

"Good question," I muttered.

Leanne's voice echoed in my head: "I cannot stress enough about how much you need to put moisturizer on your face. Your skin will get really, really dry and you will look like you have acne, especially on your face."

I had been putting lotion on my face, but it never seemed to help. I had switched to coconut oil. Don't ask me what made me think of using that; I usually added a teaspoon of it to my protein shakes, but one day, I got the idea to put it on my face instead. It seemed to be more soothing than the Eucerin. Now I would be going to church with puffy ears, a bald head, and an oily, red face.

Within weeks, the hives started. They began on my hands, traveled up my arms, crept up my neck, and hightailed it down to my legs.

I emailed Haley, "Do you think the alpha lipoic acid you prescribed is causing my new rash? It says, 'Do not take these pills if you are allergic to sulfur.' I'm allergic to sulfa drugs... or is that different?"

She assured me that the pills were fine and that I was most likely allergic to Taxol. Opinion Number One.

At my next Taxol infusion, Leanne stopped by to visit, noticed my rash, and said it was due to the Lapatinib. Opinion Number Two.

Kateri, my chemo nurse for the day, took one look at my neck and said, "What's happening with you?"

"I have a little hive problem."

"Yeah, I see that."

"It's really quite annoying."

"It doesn't look good at all. What do you think it's from?"

"Well." Where did I start? "It itches like a mad dog. Leanne thinks it's caused by the Lapatinib, Haley, I mean Dr. Burton, thinks it's caused by the Taxol, and maybe it's caused by this new pill I started taking—alpha lipoic acid."

"I'll bet that's it." Opinion Number Three.

I had seen Dr. Hoffman, the oncologist, earlier in the week. His opinion, Opinion Number Four and the one I happened to agree with, was, "What it boils down to is, we're not quite sure which one you're reacting to."

Is this what my bucket list has disintegrated to? Scratch out the dream kitchen and write, "Stop itching"?

* * *

Now that it was October, I had to contend with the pink ribbons and advertisements about Breast Cancer Awareness on top of this new rash that I couldn't control.

I was very aware that I had cancer.

First of all, I was bald as can be. I had no hair left anywhere on my body. Like I've mentioned before, it is hard to feel attractive this way. It's probably apropos for Mexican hairless dogs, but not for women.

I ate Benadryl for breakfast on a regular basis.

I was usually aware of the nearest toilet.

Nausea drove me to try marijuana and I didn't like it.

I had consumed more pain meds in the past six months than during my previous 41 years.

My social life consisted of visiting chemo nurses with my drivers.

Chemotherapy was forcing my body into early menopause and was the least of my worries.

On Halloween, our whole family was invited to a party of chili, hot chocolate, and good times. We looked forward to it all day. I decided to take a nap first; five hours later, I stumbled to the living room to find out the kids had left for the party already and Ken had stayed home with me. Like I've said before, he's a good man.

The next thing I knew, I was lying on the couch half-naked and Ken was rubbing aloe vera all over my body. While this sounds very romantic (taking advantage of the kids being out of the house and all), in reality, he was trying to prevent me from scratching the skin off my legs.

By my eighth Taxol infusion on November 12, I complained once again about the rash, had blood drawn, got pre-meds dripped into my veins, got ready for the Taxol infusion to begin, and then heard loud and clear from my liver. Apparently, the liver becomes toxic if you feed it too many poisons. On the "toxicity scale" from one to 40, mine was 326 and chemo was cancelled.

Not believing the words were coming out of my mouth, I begged the nurse, "Please, give me the Taxol anyway. I don't want to drag this out for an extra week."

When she mentioned the possibility of *permanent damage*, I thought I better zip it. I hoped my liver didn't hear how unconcerned I was for its safety.

Since my liver decided to take a slight vacation from doing its job correctly, and consequently, I got an unscheduled break from Taxol and Lapatinib, I hoped the rash would go away.

But I was still upset. The surgery, which had previously been set for May 12, postponed until January 5, and rescheduled to January 12, would now most likely be moved to January 19.

I resumed the Taxol, but Lapatinib was withheld until further notice. My liver was still upset and had the high numbers to prove it. I decided to focus on my diet.

I trudged over to my vitamin cupboard, trying to remember everything that Haley told me to do during my last appointment with her. Her handout was taped to the inside of the cupboard. The instructions said 1). Exercise every day, 2) No sugar.

No wonder my liver isn't happy with me. On top of chemo,

I feed my liver sugar daily and do no exercise.

Because of the issues with my liver and in the quest to get rid of the wretched rash, I tried everything: Coconut oil, aloe vera, Benadryl, Caladryl lotion, Eucerin, oatmeal baths, and calendula cream. I even resorted to Desitin; if it works on a baby's diaper rash, maybe it would help me, right? I guess I used too much of it. I dreamt I had a baby. Twice.

When I wasn't dreaming about babies, I was up. All night. It didn't click at first that it was because of the steroids they were giving me.

I took my liver to the doctor, two days before Thanksgiving, to get another blood test to show if there was any improvement in the level of toxicity. Alas, I would have rather taken it shopping.

My liver did not recuperate as fast as it should have from its toxic state, so while the rest of the family was grateful around the Thanksgiving table for their family, friends, school, the fireplace, and warm beds to sleep in, the biggest thing I was thankful for was: no more Lapatinib.

Chapter Fifteen
Control Freak

I'll be the first to admit it. I am a control freak.

Since the diagnosis, I noticed that my problem took off on a whole new level. Maybe I figured I couldn't control the cancer that had taken over my body and my life, so I tried to fight back in other ways. Control as many things as possible.

Now that the surgery was only 18 days away, I felt like I had the nesting urge that pregnant women go through. I was on a mission to whip the house into shape so that when I came home from the hospital, it was clean.

I thought maybe I was a bit unique in this problem of being a control freak, but then I had my friend Rose over one day. Her husband has Stage IV prostate cancer. We got to talking about house cleaning and organizing and home decorating.

She said, "You know, when Allen was first diagnosed, I went on this huge house-cleaning bender and brought piles of stuff to Goodwill. The more boxes I brought to the thrift store, the more I felt in control of life. I couldn't control my husband's cancer or his chemo, so that was how I dealt with it all."

"Oh good, I'm not crazy," I replied.

"Well, I wouldn't go that far." She grinned.

For example, I found myself saying things like, "Adriana, Michael, and Jonathan, pick up those candy wrappers and put them in the garbage. Too bad it's the most exciting part of the movie and you've had to get up six times already."

In the kitchen, I constantly reminded the kids, "*This* is the food preparation area. Do not make your toast on the dining room table. I don't care that our kitchen is only six by ten and there are four other people in there already."

Outside of the bathroom door, I knocked and yelled, "Wipe down the bathtub right away. I don't care if you're stark naked. You can get dressed later."

Back in the living room closer to bedtime, I reprimanded the kids, "When you leave the loveseat, child, put the afghan back over the leather... no, the stripes go the other way."

If Jonathan made himself a cup of hot cocoa with marshmallows, whip cream, and cinnamon, then proceeded to pick up the steaming cup in his hand, I would interrupt, "Why can't you put the cinnamon away? It goes *right there* after the allspice and basil, yes, in alphabetical order. Jonathan, don't you look at me that way."

I'm surprised sometimes that all three children don't leave home to find someone nicer to live with. If they put that on their Christmas list—find a new mother—I wouldn't have been too shocked.

Four days before Christmas, instead of doing something fun like shopping for gifts or eating lunch with a friend, I met with Haley.

"So, Maria, tell me what's happening with you."

I squirmed, but only a tiny bit because I was learning to live with my guilt. "Um, have you been reading my blog by any chance?" I sat in the chair waiting for her response. It didn't take long.

"Yes."

"I knew it."

"Eating sugar every day and not exercising, huh?"

"Well, when you put it that way. You do realize it's Christmas right now, though, right?" I asked, trying to justify my sugar consumption.

"That it is."

"And, you know that well, I realize that, hmm, that I'm not supposed to eat it, but..."

She said nothing.

I tried another tack. "Do you ever eat sugar?" There, put the onus on her for once.

"Are you kidding me? 'Do as I say and not as I do,'" she answered truthfully.

"I'm so glad. I was beginning to think you weren't human."

"Very human."

"Well, Haley, I have been cutting down on the fudge. I

only make it this time of year." Why did I admit to eating fudge? I decided to dig myself further into a hole. "Oh yeah, this fudge. It has Velveeta cheese in it. Isn't that disgusting? And I have this recipe with walnuts and peanut brittle kind of stuff and..."

I stopped. Where the heck was I going with this anyway? No wonder I was fat, unhealthy, and had cancer.

"Velveeta cheese?" she asked.

"It's the best fudge ever. I know. Tons of butter and Velveeta. Kinda gross, but my family loves it. They've got their friends hooked on it now. I won't eat any other fudge. My mom discovered it in the *Skagit Valley Herald* years ago."

Here I was paying all this money for this appointment and we were discussing recipes. What can I say? It was fun. I get into that sort of thing.

"Okay, Haley, here's the thing." I was back to justifying my bad behavior. "I know that sugar is bad for me and that I eat too much of it and it's probably in my best interest to stop eating all of this junk food."

"You're just trying to get through chemo right now."

Cool. She was helping me to justify myself.

"Here's my philosophy, though," I added. "I've eaten pretty healthy all my life and of course, while I'm not perfect, I ate healthy, exercised on a regular basis, ate all kinds of expensive vitamins, and I still ended up with cancer."

"Do you think you brought this on yourself?"

"Yeah, but that's another whole ball of wax."

"Do you want to talk about that ball of wax?"

"Not right now. Someday. What I'm talking about right now is this attitude I've been having lately."

"What's that?" she asked.

"I know that eating sugar is bad and all that, but like I said, all that healthy eating didn't do me any good. So, I think to myself, 'Screw all that; I'm going to eat whatever I want.' Pretty articulate reasoning, isn't it?"

"Okay, go on."

"Well, I have a friend who's always worried about what she eats. She does all this stuff—vitamins, this healthy diet and that healthy diet—and she still always feels under the weather. I want to scream at her: 'It's because you're always *worrying* about what you're eating. Plunk the stuff in your mouth, change your attitude, and you'll feel a heck of a lot better.' Well, I have to say that I have a really good attitude, don't you?"

She wrote down a few notes in her chart. I hoped it wasn't "This patient is crazy."

"Well, don't you think I have a good attitude?" I repeated.

"Yes, Maria, that's one thing that I notice about you. You have a good attitude most of the time. I don't always see that in my line of work."

Off I went on another tangent. Could I not just stay with the subject at hand? "About this attitude of mine. I was shopping the other day at Grocery Outlet." Seriously, who cared what store it was? That was such a bad habit of mine. Stick to the story.

"The one here in town?" she asked.

See? Now I was getting her all confused.

"No, the one down in Mount Vernon. I was shopping there and I kept passing this woman with her small child."

Really, did the small child have anything to do with it?

"Okay, go on."

"The woman and I would smile at each other a few times and then later, when I was putting my groceries in the back of my car, she came up to me and asked if I would be offended if she asked me a question. Of course, I knew she was going to ask me about my cancer. I have no hair.

"Well, to make a long story short"—this is the short version?—"this woman told me that she noticed me in the store and I looked so perky and happy. I told her, 'What do you want me to do? Lie around in bed all day, depressed and worried I'm going to die?' Of course, right after I said that, I found out that this woman had a very hard time with her own diagnosis and pretty much handled it that way."

"Make sure you continue with this good attitude. Cancer, though, is a multifactorial disease and we need to deal with a few of your health issues so that we can prevent problems down the road. When's your last Taxol infusion?"

"Tomorrow."

"That's good, right? You made it through the second leg of chemo. Now, just see if you can cut down on the sugar a bit, okay?"

I nodded and gave her the sky-blue scarf I had knitted for her for Christmas. It went perfectly with her eyes.

Celebrating Christmas was bittersweet because I didn't know if I would be around for the following one. I drowned my sorrows in Velveeta fudge, against Haley's advice, and decorating the house with my porcelain village. Adriana asked, like she does yearly, if she could have the lighted houses "when I'm dead."

On January 9, I turned 43. I resolved to celebrate ending chemotherapy and threw myself a party as if it were my 40th. I invited over a hundred people: friends I hadn't seen in a while since we switched churches, piano students, close friends, people I used to work with at the insurance company, family.

I managed to put together a slide show. I had never done that before.

We used the Allen Fire Hall, located two miles from my house. Susie did most of the work. She, Debbie, Tami, and Melissa worked tirelessly in the kitchen while I watched, flabbergasted as one after another, people came in to congratulate me. So many people.

When the slide show came on, my sister, Brenda, cried uncontrollably. "What's the problem, Brenda? Why are you crying?" I asked her.

"Looking at all those pictures, you in your wedding dress, with the kids as babies... I never showed up at chemo, not once."

Oh, the guilt-cry.

"This is a party, Brenda. Lighten up."

"Aunt Hilda was sitting next to me. She couldn't take it either."

"Snap out of it. Have fun." I could see I was still a control freak. Here I was, telling people whether or not they should cry.

The surgery loomed in five days, and I began to panic. I still didn't feel like I was prepared, mentally or physically. On one hand, I wanted it over with so I could get on with my life. But, most of the time, I was hoping for some miracle that would make the chemotherapy drugs dissolve the tumors into nothingness and I wouldn't have to do my mastectomy after all.

I needed a vacation. I realized that Ken and the kids had Martin Luther King, Jr. Day off, so I booked a one-night stay in Birch Bay.

On Sunday afternoon, I packed my clothes. We would be leaving any minute. My bathing suit was the first thing to go in. I was going to be sure to wear that as much as possible while I still had cleavage to celebrate.

When we finally arrived in Birch Bay, Ken went to check out the fitness room. The kids and I hopped into the hot tub. A couple was there ahead of us, soaking.

"I can hardly wait for Hawaii," I said to the kids. "It will be nice to swim in the ocean."

"Can we go?" Jonathan asked.

"I'll save up my own money, Mom," Michael added.

"Me, too," Adriana said.

"An anniversary trip isn't very exciting with kids, you know," was my comeback. "You guys don't really want to go to Hawaii anyway. You'd be bored."

"Beaches, pineapple, swimming; we'd be real bored," Adriana said, sarcasm dripping from her lips.

It was then that the pain hit.

I should have known. That stupid, big right toe was always causing me grief. It hurt every night during my bath. Why didn't I remember that before I tried to cram my body into this red bathing suit?

"Ow." I was so profound sometimes. What else was there to say?

"Ow, ow, ow." I guess I could say it three times in a row.

"What is it, Mommy?" Jonathan asked, concern all over his face.

"My toe." I was trying to be quiet. "Neuropathy... Ohhhhh."

Michael came to my side and put his hand under my arm. "What do you want me to do, Mom?"

I stuck my right foot out of the hot water. In the midst of my pain, I was amazed that I could sit on my butt in the hot tub and be limber enough to stick my offending appendage *out* of the water. My satisfaction was very short-lived, however, when I saw the look on the woman's face across the way.

Oh great, she thinks I have some sort of communicable foot fungus. She looks ready to bolt out of here like a hot potato.

I bolstered my mental faculties and put my foot slowly back into the water. I imagined her pinching her husband beneath the bubbles so that he would be alert to the fact that they were in the water with a freak.

My toe resisted being put back in the water. Several more moans escaped my lips, against my better judgment.

"Mom, you want me to get Dad?" Adriana offered.

"Ow, ow, ow."

So while I had managed to get my bathing suit wet (barely), it wasn't quite the relaxing time I had envisioned when I booked the vacation.

By the time we got back to reality after our short vacation and into the whirlwind of last-minute pre-op appointments (I think there were seven), I learned a lot about mastectomies and the protocol of said surgery. The thing that stands out most in my mind is what you can eat and drink the night before.

When Ken and I met with the surgeon, he explained that I was not to consume anything but clear liquids after 11:00 p.m. up until 4:00 in the morning. This meant I could have water, apple juice, tea, or black coffee. No milk, no orange juice.

He sent us over to the surgery center to pre-register. The nurse there advised, "Now, you will be able to have clear liquids until midnight."

I interrupted her. "Yippee, I get an extra hour. The doctor said eleven o'clock."

She didn't seem overly impressed with my extra hour of clear liquids and continued, "Nothing after four o'clock, okay? You will be here at seven a.m. and the surgery will be at eight o'clock."

I nodded dumbly. It was really starting to hit me. Several times, I had glibly let those words slide over my tongue without batting an eyelash: "Yeah, chemo for eight months, surgery in January." I tried to keep from hyperventilating.

The nurse turned to me and asked if there were any last-minute questions.

I flashed her a tentative smile. I only had one. "So, is vodka considered a clear liquid?"

Chapter Sixteen
Surgery

The day of reckoning had finally arrived. Thursday, January 21, 2010, a date that will forever be imprinted on my brain—that part of the brain that has not been destroyed by chemo.

I was hungry, but I ignored my grumbling stomach and rumbled around in the top drawer of the desk in my home office. With the black Sharpie pen I finally located, I wrote NOT THIS ONE on my good breast as the first order of business. I wanted to cover all my bases. Next, I made sure to have a loose-fitting zip-up jacket like Dr. Williamson had instructed. Finally, I made sure to put on lipstick like the woman in *Why I Wore Lipstick to My Mastectomy* (a great title, incidentally). I chose a bright pink shade: Jane Iredale,

Renee.

Adriana, Michael, and Jonathan were quiet on the ride up to Bellingham, where the surgery was to take place. What exactly do you say to your mother when she's about to lose a body part, even if it did allow you to take a day off from school?

Ken was quiet, too. I kept finding myself wanting to apologize to him, now that the moment was here. *I'm sorry I didn't go in to the doctor sooner, the second I discovered that lump. I'm sorry I've put this family through so much torture over the past year. I'm sorry that we might go into financial ruin over this whole thing. I'm sorry I'm losing my breast.*

We arrived at the surgery center and filled out the required intake forms.

I still couldn't believe that I was going to be in and out of the surgery center in one day. Drive-thru mastectomies? What had this world come to? It was a good thing I trusted Dr. Williamson and his method of practice.

Right before the anesthesiologist put me under, he asked me if I knew of a good piano teacher closer to his home because he was interested in taking it up as a hobby. It seemed like seconds later that the nurses told me they played Chopin in my honor while the doctor performed the surgery. I didn't tell them that Josh Groban is more my style.

In the recovery room, I kept trying to wake up, but couldn't quite manage.

"Hey, Mom," Michael poked me. "What's the name of my hat?"

"Ah," I sighed.

"Look, she's completely out of it," Jonathan nudged

Michael.

"Ask her again," Adriana instructed.

"Mom, do you know what my hat's name is?" Michael repeated.

"Ah."

Ken said, "What do you mean, Michael, what's your hat's name?"

"Oscar, Dad. Oscar the Grouch, from Sesame Street," Michael answered. He pointed to the two eyeballs hanging from green string on either side of his ears.

"Mom, what's my name?" Adriana asked.

"Ah."

"Her name is Ah. Ha ha," Jonathan said. "Mom, what's my name?" he asked.

"Ah."

Tami came to visit. I rewarded her by throwing up from the anesthetic. Nice friend I am.

"Well, Tams," Ken said, "if you're going to stay here with Maria, I'll go take the kids to lunch. They're starving."

They left the recovery room and Tami and I were left alone.

I fell asleep again.

When I awoke, a nurse was standing near my bed. "Maria, my name is Cora. Are you ready to go home?"

"What time is it?" I asked.

"Two-thirty."

I threw up again.

The nurse came back with a Coke. "Here, try this. It works better than Sprite." She deposited the can on my side table and walked away.

Blech. I was not a pop drinker.

When Ken came back from lunch, leaving the kids in the lobby, I tried to keep my eyes open and concentrate on the words coming out of his mouth.

"How's she doing?" he asked Tami.

"She just threw up again," Tami explained, "so the nurse gave her Coke."

"Coke? I thought it was Sprite that was supposed to help."

"She said Coke was better. I think they want her to go home, but I don't think she looks ready, do you?" She gestured in the general direction of my bed.

"No. She looks terrible," Ken replied.

"I'm right here, guys," I managed to croak.

Ken reached over to hold one hand and Tami held the other. My two mainstays in life.

Michael walked back into the room. "Watch this, Aunt Tami. Hey, Mom, what's the name of my hat?" Michael asked.

"What? What the heck are you talking about?"

He gestured emphatically toward the ski-style knit hat on his head. "My hat. What's it called?"

"A weird, green hat with eyeballs. What do you mean, what is it called?" I looked at Tami and she looked at me. She shrugged her shoulders.

"Don't you remember, Mom?" Michael asked.

"About what?"

"Duh. My hat. Do you remember what it's called?"

I turned to Ken for help. "What the heck is this kid talking about?"

"Every single time that the kids asked you a question right when you woke up from surgery," Ken explained, "you would reply, 'Ah.' It was hilarious."

I leaned over the end of the bed and puked into the blue bag Cora had given me along with my Coke. *Well, this isn't hilarious. I want to go home, but I don't want to move.*

It wasn't until 5:30 that I finally went home, three hours behind schedule.

I tried to get comfortable on the couch, but it was no use. My arm hurt, my chest hurt, and my stomach still felt queasy.

A visiting nurse, Charlotte, came to check on me an hour later per Dr. Williamson's request.

"Is this normal, Charlotte, for women to have mastectomies and be home the same day?" Ken asked her.

"Actually, it's not around here, but I've dealt with Dr. Williamson's patients before and they always seem to get back on their feet faster than those who stay in the hospital. From what I understand, he's light years ahead of the pack. He'll be working on research well before other people get around to the same thing years later."

Ken's shoulders relaxed.

I sat on the couch, trying not to move while she checked my bandages and drainage tubes.

"Everything looks good here. Another nurse will be by tomorrow to check on you, okay?"

I nodded.

Ken helped me to our bed after Charlotte had gone home. I lay down on my left side and Ken tucked a pillow up close to my chest to replace the hunk of flesh they had taken from my body earlier. I draped my arm over the pillow carefully.

I tossed and turned most of the night because I kept feeling like I was going to roll over and fall on my face in spite of the pillow. I felt disoriented and off-kilter. The nausea wasn't helping.

Friday night, I was able to sleep a bit more than the night before because of sheer exhaustion.

Saturday morning, I took a bath just before the third visiting nurse arrived. Barbara was very professional as she listened to my heart, lungs, and bowels, took my blood pressure and temperature, drained the tubes, and checked the bandages.

"I was so proud of myself yesterday, Barbara. I baked bread and did some knitting." I held up a scarf.

Barbara put her blood pressure cuff and thermometer away.

"I think my arm's a bit swollen, Barbara."

"Well, honey, you overdid it yesterday with your knitting and bread-baking. That scarf is beautiful and everything, but it's only been two days. Give yourself a break. Make sure to keep your arm elevated above your heart a couple times today, okay?"

I nodded.

Barbara was sweet with her gentle admonition to "take it easy." The main word of professional advice she had for me, however, was, "Today, you must have a poopie."

Chapter Seventeen
Post-Surgery

I continued to pound down the Vicodin, even though I knew it could interfere with my "poopies."

I started having strange dreams. Was that another side effect?

Detective Eames from *Law & Order* and I were running from a gun-toting bear in a park and decided to walk to Disneyland instead. Either I had a deep-seated wish to go back to Disneyland again or I had been watching a few too many *Law & Order: Criminal Intent* episodes during my time on the couch.

After I was done running around Disneyland, I started dreaming on a more local level. As a family, we moved to a parking lot in town and I was lying in a sleeping bag on the ground three feet from a busy road. When I moved to safety, I had to walk over a bunch of red-hot coals to get to the inside of the house. That was an easy one to interpret. The spot where my right breast used to be felt like it was on fire.

* * *

Tired and restless from being housebound, I longed to go out in public. By the time I actually had some place to go, though, six days after the surgery, I came to the conclusion that I was more self-conscious about the amount of hair on my head than the fact that my right breast was missing. I hemmed and hawed about whether or not to wear a scarf on my head to my get-together with the writing group.

I combed my hair, wet it, and debated about mousse-ing it. I took out a hand mirror and looked at the back of my head in the bathroom mirror. There just wasn't enough hair there to make me feel comfortable. I felt like a boy.

I remembered the conversation I'd had with Tami the day before.

"Maria, I don't know why you can't get it through your thick skull. You look great without those scarves or hats. You look sexy. Just take the dumb things off and go out without them. You have a nice-shaped head, so flaunt it. I told you: you remind me of Jamie Lee Curtis."

"Now, if only I had her body to go with it, eh?"

"Ain't that the truth."

Susie drove me to Coupeville and went shopping while I made my way down to the coffee shop at the end of the pier, carefully, since I was about due for another Vicodin. A literary agent from California that I had met earlier was up and it was great to see him again, along with the rest of the writers in the group.

Andrea, the founder of this free writing class, spoke. "Let's go around the table and introduce ourselves and say what we're planning on working on today."

I plan on not throwing up when it's my turn to talk... please, don't let me throw up in public, especially in front of Gordon; he just got here from California.

A woman I had never met said, "If Marie can come here one week after having surgery, I have no excuses for not working on my flash fiction."

I should have stayed home.

On the way home, I turned to Susie. "Ew, I think I'm going to throw up," I moaned.

"Go ahead," Susie said, quite calm under the circumstances. "I'm not worried about the car."

"I am. I'm worried about me, too. Oh, I don't feel good." I reached into my purse. Two Mentos. An hour drive. I would have to make them last.

My first day out and back in the real world was very draining. That night, I continued dreaming. I was shot by an insurance salesman and had only 10 hours left to live (don't ask me how I knew that, but that's the way it goes in dreams). I said goodbye to my kids, and then instinctively knew that DiNozzo and Abby from *NCIS* were going to do an autopsy on me and I wanted to give them some clues as to who my killer was.

The next day, my mom came over to clean the house. Charlotte, the visiting nurse who had attended to me the first night home from surgery, sat next to me on the couch and said, "You do realize that your body needs rest in order to repair, right? I'm sure it was important for you to go to your writing group, but give yourself more time."

I couldn't even argue with her.

My mom picked up around us and listened to our conversation.

Charlotte took out her laptop and made herself comfortable on my leather couch. "You have a prosthesis, right?"

"No. Dr. Williamson told me not to wear a bra for at least a month, so, I'm letting them swing. I mean, it."

"It says here in the computer that you have a prosthesis." She corrected the information and then said, "Last time I got fitted for a bra, I switched to a size G."

"I didn't know bras came in that size," my mom volunteered.

"Yeah," Charlotte answered, "my friends always tease me that it's G for gigantic, but I tell them it's G for gorgeous."

"Well, I used to be a double D," I said. "Am I just a D now? One boob, one D."

My mom cackled.

"People used to tell me I was lucky for having big boobs," I continued. "I always come back and tell them that I have a big butt and stomach to go with it, so what's the big deal? I'd rather have small everything."

Of course, no one ever dares tease me about big breasts anymore since I only have one left.

Chapter Eighteen
Follow-Up

A week and a half after the surgery, Ken and I met with Dr. Williamson.

"Well, the good news is that a mastectomy was the right choice for you due to the spread of cancer we found. Four out of the eleven lymph nodes we removed tested positive for cancer."

"Four out of eleven's not bad," I said, forever the optimist.

"Maria, that's four out of eleven *after* chemo, which means we will want you to do radiation."

Shit.

"When do you start Herceptin?" Dr. Williamson asked. He rifled through his notes.

"Tomorrow." *My life is never going to be my own again.*

While Herceptin was not considered chemotherapy by the nurses and doctors, I still had to go to the infusion center every three weeks, have the drug administered via the portacath, and have my heart checked regularly because there was a chance of heart damage.

Heart damage sounded tame compared to the one sentence my eyes honed in on the one time I allowed myself to look at a Herceptin brochure: *Fatal infusions have been reported.* Why would I want to receive such a treatment? Oh yeah, because I had HER2/neu breast cancer.

HER2/neu breast cancer patients are reported to have a worse prognosis and increased disease recurrence than those women who do not have this protein in their blood. I had watched part of a Lifetime movie once about the man who invented Herceptin. This was, of course, before I needed it myself.

The chemo nurses had told me during my last Taxol infusion that this drug was a cakewalk compared to all previous treatments I had received thus far.

A week after my first Herceptin infusion, which was *not* fatal, Ken and I had a consult set up to see the radiologist. Ken had a cup of coffee while I grabbed the first intake form and proceeded to fill it out.

"Sudden loss of weight?" *I wish.*

"Sudden gain of weight?" Now that was more like it.

"Hot flashes?" I hadn't had one of those in a few weeks so I left it blank.

"Chance of pregnancy?" That was one way to get out of radiation. Probably wouldn't be fair to the kid.

Ken and I were ushered into Dr. Jergen's office where we were told we'd get to see a film in a few moments. I wished desperately that we were watching *Extraordinary Measures* with Harrison Ford instead, holding hands and eating popcorn. I just knew with all the busyness, I was going to miss that movie while it was still out in theaters.

The nurse took my blood pressure. "One-sixteen over seventy. That's very good."

"That's the only number I have that's consistently good. The weight's always too high, my liver's too high, the white blood count is too low, the red blood count is too high, let's see... what else? I guess the temperature is always normal. I still can't believe I weigh 222.2 pounds. Insane."

After she had noted down all the pertinent information, she cued up the movie *How Radiation Works*, brought to us by Siemens. Ken and I sat, nervously, *not* holding hands, while I sucked on Wilhelmina candies and drank Stash peppermint tea like there was no tomorrow.

Dr. Jergens came in. He seemed like a happy fellow. He had thinning gray hair and small-framed glasses.

Ken piped up almost immediately, "Dr. Jergens, Maria's not real thrilled about doing radiation. She said she didn't want to do chemo and I had to drag her kicking and screaming through that. She's more of a natural kind of girl. Naturopaths, vitamins, that sort of thing."

I interrupted. "It's not like anyone *wants* to do radiation—or chemo for that matter."

The doctor picked up on my cue. "I was just going to say that." He took out the pathology report and looked down at it. "So, you're at T3, LN1, M0."

I could see he had lost Ken.

"That's Stage III, lymph node involvement, and no metastases. I would recommend that you do twenty-eight treatments."

I tried to add it up in my head. Leanne had already told me it would be anywhere from six to eight weeks.

Twenty-eight... divided by... only a couple days a week... Monday through Thursday? Friday... this dang-blasted chemo brain... twenty-eight..."

"It works out to eight weeks total." I see his brain was working fine.

"There's a problem," I said bluntly. "We have a vacation booked for April. Is that going to be an issue?" I tried to keep the touch of defiance out of my voice, but, really, it was no secret that I did not want to be here.

"Well..."

"Listen, half treatment is better than no treatment at all." No treatment was sounding better and better, especially since I watched the Siemens film.

Dr. Jergens looked at the calendar. He explained that I would have to wait six weeks from the surgery, which meant I would have to do the radiation during March and April.

"Of course, vacations are very important to people going through treatment for cancer," Dr. Jergens said. He shoved his glasses up on his nose.

"It wouldn't hurt my family any, either. They've all had a rough go of it, every last one of them." I almost pointed to Ken, who was slouched in his chair, and said, "See? Look at the poor man. He's at the end of his rope."

"Yes, we could arrange that." Smart doctor. He knew

that if he said no, I'd most likely bolt out the door and out of his life forever.

All of a sudden, a hot flash swept over me in a wave. "Whoo-eeeee, it's hot in here. Guess I should have marked hot flashes as a 'yes' on that form."

Dr. Jergens recommended I make an appointment for two weeks from that day and we shook hands all around. I stood up and took off the gown that the nurse had pressed into my hand. The doctor never even examined me. How could he? I still had the darn bandages on.

I felt another wave come over me. This time it was not a hot flash, but a wave of nausea.

"I need a peppermint right now," I warned Ken. "My tea is gone. Maybe they have hot water here, but I think all the goodness has been zapped out of the tea bag already. Oh, we have to go. Now."

The nurse made another appointment for me while Ken got some hot water from the lobby and poured it into my travel mug.

In the Honda, I shoved a peppermint in my mouth.

"Ken, those nurses told me Herceptin was a cakewalk compared to Taxol. I think they were lying." I pressed my face against the cool window and murmured, "Cakewalk, cakewalk, cakewalk...."

I had only had one Herceptin infusion so far, almost a week ago, and today was definitely the worst for the amount of nausea I was feeling.

"Mer, is there anything I can do?"

"Get home fast. Oh, this is a cakewalk alright: devil's food cake."

Chapter Nineteen
Sex Oil

February 11 and it was finally time to take out the drainage tubes I still carted around with me everywhere. I sat in the surgeon's waiting room, waiting for the Vicodin I had saved up for the occasion to kick in.

Debbie turned to me, knitting needles poised in mid-air. "I think I only have 32 stitches now. I'm supposed to have 34, right?"

"Take it out," I commanded. "I'm going to teach you how to knit the correct way."

I was glad for the distraction. I took the knitting needles from Debbie and carefully took the yarn off. Her eyes grew wide.

“It’s okay,” I reassured her. “You have to learn how to correct your mistakes. It’s the best way to learn.”

“Maria de Haan.” I looked up to see Dr. Williamson standing in the doorway. Debbie grabbed her knitting from me, and shoved it into her bag. I picked up the Tupperware container of Kip cereal Debbie had brought to help me keep the Vicodin in my stomach, and we followed the doctor into the exam room.

He inspected the tubes as I babbled on and on nervously: “I think Tube Number 2 was kinked because for a couple of days it didn’t have any stuff in it and the Tube Number 1, which usually had nothing, all of a sudden had a whole bunch of fluid in it and then when I noticed it and fixed it, Tube Number 1 all of a sudden had nothing in it again and Tube Number 2 had a bunch in it again and it really hurt last night and the day before and I think it’s because the skin is trying to heal around it and I keep kinking it on accident and...”

I’m sure he wanted to muzzle me. I knew I was talking too much but I was afraid it was going to hurt when he removed the tubes. Even more, I was worried he was only going to take out one of the tubes and not the other.

Sure enough, a few seconds later, he said, “Well, you kinked the drain and you pulled it, but I think we can take the other one out.”

“Noooooo. I want them both out.”

He loosened the belt that held the drains to my body and held it up in front of me. “Do you want this?”

“I don’t ever want to see that thing again.”

“Okay, I’d like you to lie down.” He helped me.

Debbie stood behind him, ready to check out all the action. She sure was more daring than I was. I wouldn't want to see someone else get their bandages removed. I could hardly look at my own.

Dr. Williamson turned to her. "You'll have to sit down."

He began inspecting the dressing. "Did part of this bandage come off?"

"Not that I know of."

"You definitely pulled on this."

"Not on purpose. It must have happened while I was sleeping or when I was milking the tube."

"Well, it definitely pulled."

"That would explain a lot." The pain the night before had been excruciating.

I peeked beneath his arm while he stood next to me and saw Debbie's face. The look on her face cracked me up. He had told her to sit down but she still managed to sneak a look at what he was doing. She was obviously fascinated with his handiwork. Personally, I was sick of his handiwork and wanted to get on with my life.

He kept poking and prodding. I wished I had taken an extra Vicodin and tried not to cry.

"You know," I said through gritted teeth, "yesterday I went to my kids' basketball games and they had this fundraiser for cancer and this girl came up to me and asked if I wanted to donate a dollar. I kind of ripped her head off and said, 'I've donated a lot of money to cancer already.' Poor thing. It wasn't really her fault. I'm not even sure she got what I meant."

"I'm sure it was fine," Dr. Williamson reassured me.

"You know what else? It kills me how they use soda pop and cupcakes to try to help fund research for cancer. They should sell carrots." I was in a foul mood.

"I agree with you," Dr. Williamson said.

"You do?" I was surprised. "You know what else? I think walk-a-thons in the name of cancer are a complete waste of time. Instead of having people walking around in circles, why don't people volunteer at infusion centers or knit hats or something useful?"

"I totally agree with that, too," Dr. Williamson said. "I don't think people realize that all the money goes to some place in Atlanta, Georgia and doesn't help local research at all."

"I think it's great that cancer survivors want to get together. Don't get me wrong," I said. "Just don't charge money for it and put your time to better use somewhere else. I dread the day someone asks me to do one of those, because I won't do it. I'd rather write a book or make a quilt or volunteer at the infusion center someday. Right now, I wish I could stop going there."

A few moments later, he said, "Okay, it won't hurt when I take the tubes out; it will just feel a little bit funny." He removed them and then started in on all the bandages. One after the other, he took them off and threw them in the garbage. I didn't look. Debbie did enough looking for the two of us.

As each bandage came off, I felt more and more free. It was very short-lived, however. He applied a fresh bandage and helped me back up to a sitting position.

"You play piano, right?" he asked.

"Yep."

"Well, not for the next three days you won't."

"Pardon me?"

"You will do *nothing* for the next three days."

I looked at him, shocked. What did he mean by that? I was free, free, free at last. Why couldn't I start walking and get some of the weight I had gained back off?

"I'm supposed to see the naturopath tomorrow." He heard the question in my voice and shook his head no.

"What about doing dishes?"

"Nope."

"What about church on Sunday?"

"Nothing."

"Can I knit?" I wasn't going to give up that easily.

"Knitting should be okay if you're very careful. Let me explain. If you move your arm too much in the next 72 hours, you will cause fluid to build up on the chest wall and then I will have to aspirate it with a needle."

"Well, why didn't you just say that in the first place?"

* * *

By February 17, it was time to take the rest of the staples out. Ken came with me this time.

When Dr. Williamson walked in, he asked if there was any swelling.

"I don't think so. I sat around and did nothing. Except knit. Boy, did I knit."

Dr. Williamson slowly peeled off the bandages and removed the rest of the staples.

"I can hardly wait to take a shower," I commented.

"Maria, you might want to be prepared for the emotional aspect of this whole ordeal. Several women have a hard time with that first shower, looking down and noticing that their breast is missing."

"I'm more self-conscious about the lack of hair on my head."

"I want you to still be aware that this is something that might happen to you. I had a patient yesterday who was out with her girlfriends and one of them made the comment about her 'having cancer' and she flipped out and screamed at her friend that she used to have cancer and she didn't have it anymore. She was so shocked at her reaction because it wasn't the way she normally would have reacted."

"I kind of think it would have hit me already, but I'll pay attention."

He explained the few exercises I needed to start doing: walking my fingers up the wall as high as possible 10 times in a row straight-on and again from the side.

"When will I get the rest of the bandages off?"

"I'm giving your body back to you. You can do whatever you want with it now."

"What I'd like to do is lose 60 pounds overnight and look like Jamie Lee Curtis. Any chance of that?"

When we were done at Dr. Williamson's, Ken and I crossed town and met with Haley.

"You know, Maria, I'm still reading your blog. You really need to cut down on the amount of sugar you eat."

"I'm not exercising either. I sit on the couch and knit. Hours on end."

"You really need to concentrate on eating dark fruit and garlic and onions... as many fruits and vegetables as you can. You need to exercise."

"You know, Haley, the other day, I made cream puffs because Michaela—one of my piano students and the daughter of the guy who redid my bathroom—was coming over to play Rook." Here I went again, off topic. What did Michaela and Rook have to do with anything? "I picked one of those hummers up and began psycho-analyzing it: *This little morsel of goodness could actually kill me? Do I care?* I used to have a positive attitude about this whole cancer business. This past week, however, I'm getting a bit pessimistic about it.

"Of course, I don't wish cancer upon all my easygoing friends; I'm just trying to weigh the fact that I know sugar is not exactly *good* for me versus the fact that Trader Joe's' dark chocolate-covered caramels just plain make me happy."

Ken spoke. "You know, Haley, I dragged her through chemo kicking and screaming and now, I have to do the same thing with radiation."

"I already told you that you could do whatever you want to when you get cancer," I shot back. "I know I'm stubborn. I'm also sick and tired of doing all this stuff."

Ken said, "One time, during chemo, I remember asking her what she thought about all this cancer business and she said that she thought it would kill her. I kind of forgot about that until just now."

I looked at him in shock. "I never said that."

"Yes, you did. I'm positive."

Haley jumped into the conversation. "This is what I'm

talking about, Maria. You need to be in this one hundred percent and take charge of your health. Every time you feel like eating that Häagen-Dazs ice cream, the caramels, or bingeing on some other candy, you need to think about how it's going to affect your overall health."

I changed the subject. "Neuropathy. Does it affect other parts of the body besides fingers and toes?"

She looked at me with a blank look.

I continued. "The other night, Ken and I were, well, you know, and sometimes, I think that the neuropathy affects me there, too."

"Oh," she said, her eyebrows rising in consternation.

I imagined Ken was holding his breath, wondering what crazy thing was going to come out of my mouth next.

The room was silent for a few moments, and then Haley said, "You do realize you just had major surgery and you're still sore, right?"

"Yes. But, still."

"I have not heard of that problem."

"I did a bit of research on the Internet—I know Google's not always reliable—and apparently it is a problem."

Ken fidgeted in his seat.

"Have you tried K-Y Jelly?" Haley asked.

"That's not it. I'm not dry."

"Do you think it could be from menopause?" she asked.

"I don't know. I just can't always *feel*. It seems to come and go. I guess it could be a bit from menopause," I conceded. "But I'm not really in menopause yet, am I? I could always use coconut oil if it ever comes to that. I can see it now. Every time Ken walks by a coconut in Hawaii, he'll be saying, 'Hey, is that coconut I smell?'" I pretended to sniff like a dog.

Both Haley and I said at the same time, "Just like Pavlov's dogs."

The coconut comment seemed to give her an idea. "I wonder if the girls from Living Earth Herbs would like an assignment. They could put together some sort of mixture for you with coconut oil in it."

It was several weeks later when Haley called me at home. Talk about excellent service.

"Well, I talked to Living Earth Herbs and they have a bottle for you."

We started giggling.

"When I first called them, they were *so* excited to be handed such a project. Usually, they're putting oils together for things like arthritis or gout."

Great, they're all laughing at me. Oh well, my modesty went out the window such a long time ago already.

"Well, I'm glad... I... could... oblige." What else was I supposed to say?

"They haven't named the oil yet, so if you think of anything, let them know."

"We don't exactly want to call it 'Marie de Haan's Sexual Dysfunction Oil,' do we?"

"The boss talked to the employees and told them all to take it home and test it out. They were all really excited about it."

"I'll bet they were. Boy, I really wish I could blog about it," I said. "I've already written about boobs, poop, and all kinds of other embarrassing things. I think this might be a bit much, though."

"You're probably right," she agreed. "Just give them a call and when they decide that it smells and tastes good, they'll let us know."

"Hey," I cut in, "even though I don't think I could put it in the blog, there's no reason I can't put it in the book someday, right?" My goodness, how far I had fallen.

"Great idea."

"I have to be able to talk about sex, too, on top of everything, right? It's part of life. It used to be anyway."

Chapter Twenty
Boob Shopping

Inspired to eat healthy after my last conversation with Haley, I swung by the Skagit Valley Food Co-op on my way to pick up Jonathan from school. You know the type of place—the one where people in dreadlocks and "Moses sandals" shop. I found a heavy, healthy looking red cabbage and put it in the basket with the rest of my healthy purchases. No sugar in any way, shape, or form.

At the checkout, I watched the numbers flash by on the screen. "That cabbage was eight dollars?" I asked the checker politely, when what I wanted to do was hop on the counter and yell at the top of my lungs, "Hush-a-kree'-ness!" which is a Dutch word that basically means holy crap.

If I hadn't been late already, I would have returned the

cabbage to the refrigerated section. Instead, I made my way toward school.

Two miles from school, a man in a pickup careened from the side street to my right, directly across my path. He had to have been going 40 miles per hour and apparently, stop signs didn't mean anything to him.

I fumed, *I survived six months of brutal chemotherapy to be taken out by a jerk like you?*

There were several times over the past six months that I wondered to myself if life was even worth living, not a typical thought process for me. I felt apathetic and had a hard time getting motivated to do anything.

Now, as I saw my life flash before my eyes in the glinting of the sun on the taillight of the truck that had whizzed past me, I thought of all the things I wanted to do with my life before it was all taken away from me.

My book. How would I get it written, much less published and on the bookshelves, if I got in a fatal car crash now?

What about Hawaii? It was important to me to go there with Ken. Although we got along for the most part, our marriage had had its ups and downs. A few times, over the years, we had discussed divorce, but neither one of us ever made it to a lawyer.

Cancer seemed to strengthen our marriage. The sex oil wasn't hurting it any, either.

"Hm, is that cinnamon I smell?" Ken had asked the night before. He was massaging some over my back and shoulder. Both were sore from trying to find a comfortable position to sleep in every night.

"I think so," I replied. "Supposed to add heat to the mixture."

"What's all in here anyway?"

"Cinnamon, coconut oil... lavender, maybe? I can't remember everything they put in there."

"We'll have to take this on our trip to Hawaii."

"Do you think we'll really be able to swing that trip, Ken? I feel guilty. People from church donated money to our medical bills, our tuition got paid by three other people. How can we even think about going to Hawaii?"

"You booked that room for $33, right?"

"Yeah. I ended up using all our timeshare points from this year and next year. The $33 was just the tax."

"Mer, we're going on that trip. I keep checking flights. If they keep going down, I'm going to book two airline tickets."

"Keep rubbing. That feels good," I murmured.

"I aim to please."

"Sitting on the beach in Maui. I won't believe it until my toes are curled in the sand, Ken. Remember how white the sand is there?"

"Yep."

"I gotta get to Nordstrom's and get my prosthesis."

"Where's that coming from?"

"We're going to Hawaii. I want to be prepared. I wonder if they make special bathing suits?"

"I'm sure they do."

* * *

On March 18, I met with the oncologist.

"Hi, Dr. Hoffman, what are we talking about today?"

"How's the book coming along?"

"Still plugging away on it. You know, I'm going back through some of the notes I took while I was taking Vicodin. I don't know what I was talking about half the time."

"Well, I see you had another echocardiogram yesterday." Then he began to speak German: "It looks like you have mild global left ventricular dysfunction with estimated EF 45-50%, trace mitral and tricuspid regurgitation. When compared to echo of 1/2010, LV function appears reduced."

"What... does that... mean... exactly?"

"It means that since January, your heart function has decreased and I am not giving you any more Herceptin until I determine if it's irreversible or not."

"Ah, English." I felt like responding with another choice Dutch word, one I had heard my dad use on more than one occasion when he was mad at us as children. Would this madness ever end?

* * *

Tami and I had a rare moment where we actually got together somewhere other than the infusion center. We looked at cameras at Costco and then ended up in the bar at Red Robin.

Halfway through our meal, I asked her, "Hey, you want to go boob shopping with me?"

This is probably not something you want to say too loudly in a bar, but this is how blunt and immodest I've become. She didn't even look at me funny, but knew exactly what I meant and readily agreed.

We planned to meet on Friday. Before she arrived, I went to the computer to blog about the momentous occasion:

> I haven't shopped at Nordstrom (very ritzy store) for a long time. I've got my Prada purse (Goodwill for $4.00) and $500 Calvin Klein red wool coat ($80 from Ross) and will be leaving any minute (five, to be exact) to meet Vern (best friend) to drop off her kid (cutest kid in the world) at her mom's (one of my drivers). My appointment to be fitted for lingerie (new bra) is at 12:00 (noon) and I plan on purchasing—as advertised on their website—a mastectomy product (fake boob).

"Hey, Tami," I said, on the way down to Seattle, "I read on the Nordstrom website that they sell 'mastectomy products.' Isn't that funny?"

"I read your blog this morning. That cracked me up."

"Let's pretend we're out shopping for the day, okay? Don't you miss all the fun things we used to do? Running around downtown Mount Vernon in the fall, looking for dishes at Gretchen's, going to lunch at Mexico Café? Instead, here we are on the way to a fancy store, ready to get a piece of plastic or rubber to replace the part they cut out of my body. I guess it is what it is. I'm glad I'm finally getting it done."

As we entered the lingerie department, I felt a twinge of nostalgia. Shopping for a sexy piece of lace would never be the same. Sex oil was all fine and dandy, but there was something about these undergarments that made me wish the surgery had never happened.

"Come on, Vern. Let's see if we can find where we're supposed to be."

As if in answer to my confusion, a friendly-looking salesperson walked up to us. "Hi, I'm Melissa. I'll be helping you today." Boy, they had good service at Nordstrom.

The three of us filtered into a dressing room the size of my kitchen. Tami sat on the bench, which bordered one end of the room. I stood, while Melissa efficiently took my measurements.

After I had removed my twelfth bra, I took out the new prosthesis, handed it to Tami and said, "Hey, Vern, can you hold my boob, please?" The dressing room next door was suddenly very quiet.

Oops.

Chapter Twenty-One
One Year and Counting

One year since my diagnosis. I couldn't believe it.

Last year, at this time, we drove to California for the family's spring break vacation. This year, we spent it on the Oregon coast with David, Debbie, Olivia, and Abigail. There are worse ways to mark time.

I wonder where I'll be next year at this time. California again? Hawaii with the whole family? In the hospital with a spread of cancer to my brain? One place I'd rather not go right now is heaven. Sure, I want to go there eventually, but not right this second.

That's where I thought I was headed on Sunday during our vacation. It was Jonathan's birthday and Ken and I wanted to spend some time alone with him before the whole group took him out for his birthday dinner later. On this day of rest, the three of us went hiking along the hills near the beach. I thought I was going to have a heart attack on the spot.

Dr. Hoffman had warned me that my heart wasn't working properly because of the Herceptin. I'm sure being completely out of shape didn't help.

It seemed surreal that it had been a whole year since I sat in the gynecologist's office to hear that I had "advanced" breast cancer. A lot of things had happened over the course of the year, some good, some bad.

Being in Oregon with David and Debbie and their family was definitely a good thing. The vacation was clouded, however, by the private war I held with myself over whether or not I wanted to continue the fight to live or not, especially in regard to radiation.

"Ken," I whispered one night in our condo, when all the kids had gone to bed, "you still think I should do radiation, don't you?"

"Yes. Dr. Williamson and Dr. Hoffman both said you should do it. They're the experts."

"I know. But Haley didn't seem wild about the idea."

"She didn't say one way or the other."

"She said it can cause blood cancers."

"That's not a given," he countered.

"It was for Terri, my cousin. I thought all these years that her breast cancer turned into leukemia, but when I said that to Dr. Williamson at that first appointment, he said that it was really an 'unfortunate side effect of the chemo.' Do you remember that?"

"Yes. It doesn't mean that it's going to happen like that for you."

"I know that."

"Ria told me that ever since she had radiation, she hasn't been able to sing in church. She can never catch her breath. While I'm not the best singer around, I like to do it. Life's too short not to sing, don't you think?" Ria was a friend of mine who had moved across the mountains several years before. When she found out about my cancer, she was diligent about emailing and calling to encourage me, since she was old-hat with the experience.

"I want you to live, Mer. I want you to see Adriana grow up and get married."

"What about Michael and Jonathan?"

"Them, too."

"Will you support me, though, if I choose not to do radiation?"

"I will, but I'm begging you to think about this decision more carefully."

"One year, Ken. It's been one year since this all started. I can't take much more of it."

"I know." He gave me a hug because I started crying. I couldn't help myself.

When we arrived home from our vacation, it was time to think about going on a date with my husband.

"Are you awake?" Ken called me from work one morning at six.

"Well, I am now," I replied groggily.

"What time is your heart appointment?"

"One forty-five."

"I'll pick you up around one."

"Okay."

This is what our dating has disintegrated to: going to another echocardiogram together to see if the damage from the Herceptin was permanent or not. I can sure think of a lot more fun things to do than that.

At one forty-five, Ken and I were ushered into the white, sterile room.

"Hi, I'm Rachel," the technician said. "Maria, I need you to take everything off from the waist up. I'll be right on the other side of this curtain, okay?"

I nodded. Ken sat in the chair next to the examining table.

I was having a hard time taking my bra off because the prosthesis was so heavy and my arm was sore from rototilling the garden. I coyly turned my back toward Ken and said, "Hey, why don't you unclasp my bra for me and pretend we're having a good time?"

Rachel laughed heartily on the other side of the curtain. "You two sound like you're having a good time."

"Wait until we go to Maui!" I exulted. I could hardly wait.

* * *

It was time to see Haley again.

"Okay, let's have you step on the scale first."

I had made sure to go to the bathroom first, and now I removed my shoes, took my coat off, and sure enough, I had still gained seven pounds. I *knew* I had partied a little too hard on our trip to the Oregon coast and all that chocolate was now biting me in the butt, literally. "Hey, I could always take my new boob out... that's got to be good for four pounds, don't you think?" I asked.

"Oh, you got it?" She must have felt comfortable with me because she hopped right out of her chair and placed *both* hands on either side of my right breast and said, "Cool." Then again, I must feel comfortable, too, because I let her and didn't think anything of it... until I looked out the window, that is.

You have to realize, her office is surrounded by high-rise buildings. "Hey, Haley, you do know that if anyone over there was looking in, they'd get an eyeful right now."

I guess she really did abide by the naturopath's mantra: *Treat the whole person.* She just took it a little more seriously than others.

Another person who took my medical care a bit too seriously was the clinical trial nurse, Leanne. She came to visit me during my third Herceptin infusion. Susie and I sat visiting when Leanne sat down on the other side of me.

"How is the radiation going, Maria?"

I instantly felt the hackles rise on the back of my neck. Leanne knew I wasn't doing radiation because I had stumbled across an email between her and Ken discussing the fact that I didn't want to do it.

I resented her pretending to engage me in a pleasant conversation. We were talking about matters of life and death here—literally—and I was sick of thinking about this subject.

"Oh, I've elected not to do radiation, Leanne," I said, as

sweet as pie. Two could play at this game.

"What? Radiation is standard treatment. You will be yanked off the clinical trial for being noncompliant."

"Leanne," I continued, "we both know that this trial is testing the difference between patients having Lapatinib and Herceptin versus those having one or the other alone." Did she think she could pull one over on me? What happened to her soothing voice? I loved that soothing voice. And she had done so many other nice things for me. I know she meant well, but it still irked me that this was happening.

"It's standard treatment," she repeated.

Why didn't she just call me an idiot to my face in front of all the other nurses and sick patients while she was at it?

Susie quietly cut in, "I think Maria discussed this issue with her doctor." She was sweet. She was trying to help me out of this awkward situation.

"Oh, Leanne, guess what?" I said. "I got my new prosthesis from Nordstrom." I did an about-face. "Yep, went from a size double D to a size G. Can you believe it?"

She stared at me.

"Yeah, the lady who helped me was really nice." Maybe you could take some lessons from her, I wanted to add. I had thrown her off-guard. I think she wanted me to wilt under her gaze and I wasn't going to budge.

"Maria," she began again, her voice getting louder with each sentence, "you were supposed to start that radiation several weeks ago. It's probably too late to start it now."

I felt a small niggle of uncertainty. What if she was right? What if my decision was the wrong one and ended with a coffin and my family and friends gathered around wailing,

"If she had only done that radiation"?

It's not like we were picking out shoes here. Or even a different-sized boob to replace the one that I had recently had removed from my body.

Somehow, cancer was making me assertive in ways I never thought possible.

"Leanne, the surgeon said doing radiation would only add three percent to the odds that this breast cancer will not kill me. That number is not big enough for me."

"What does he know?"

Okay, she was really ticking me off now. "Oh, he's only been a doctor for 32 years, specializing in breast cancer, and he didn't give me a hard time like you are."

I didn't say this to her, of course. Instead, I said, "I need to have Dr. Hoffman fill out this paper for the nice lady at Nordstrom for insurance purposes." I handed her the crumpled paper out of my purse.

Her face flushed red with anger. "Standard treatment."

By this time, I wanted to stand up on my chair and yell, "I'm an exceptional patient! Dr. Bernie Siegel would be proud and applaud my admirable bravery! I have my own brain and I don't have to do what you say!"

The only problem was, I was strapped to my Herceptin IV bag and couldn't move. Besides, there were sick people all around us and I refused to stoop to her level. "Leanne," I said firmly, "if I made the wrong decision here, *I* will be the one to ultimately pay for this decision with my life. It will affect you in no way whatsoever."

When I returned home from that appointment, I contacted Leanne's supervisor and quietly, calmly, and reasonably pulled out of the clinical trial. I had made my decision.

Hawaii was coming up in one short month. I planned on forgetting all about radiation and Leanne's disapproval. I was going to spend my 20th wedding anniversary with my husband who had been through hell right along with me.

Chapter Twenty-Two
The Marie/Maria Project

I finally watched *Julie & Julia* with Adriana. I had given the DVD to her for Christmas and we were just now getting around to watching it. What can I say? I'd been a little busy with Herceptin, doctor appointments, and writing a book.

If you haven't seen this movie, it is based on the true story of a woman named Julie who blogged about tackling Julia Child's *Mastering the Art of French Cooking*. She dubbed her endeavor the Julie/Julia Project: "524 recipes in 365 days." She had a counter on the website (according to the movie, anyway) to keep herself accountable.

Maybe I should do that with my weight: "67 pounds in 10 years." Sometimes, I think that's how long it will take me.

It sure wouldn't hurt me to lose weight. They say that women who have breast cancer and are overweight have a worse prognosis. I already had the HER2/neu angle against me.

One thing I had going for me was my good attitude. Then again, I was starting to think I was schizophrenic and the good attitude was just a hoax:

Marie: "I *can* lose 50 pounds in five months."

Maria: "Who are you kidding? You can't lose five pounds to save your life."

Marie: "I've consumed 1,500 calories per day all week. Be positive."

Maria: "You still gained four pounds. Why should you bother?"

Marie: "Maybe it was just water retention."

Maria: "*I'm* going to eat whatever I want this week and you can't stop me."

Marie: "Oh look, I lost four pounds again eating junk food. What?"

Maria: "I rest my case."

Ken and I went to see Dr. Hoffman, but not for my schizophrenic tendencies.

"Maria, your heart test came back normal again, so I see that we resumed your Herceptin."

"Yes, that infusion was not very pleasant. I don't think Leanne was very happy about my choice to not do the radiation. Oh yeah, speaking of happy, I wanted to let you know that I have you down as Dr. Happy in my book. What do you think about that?"

"I don't think much about that at all. You can call me Clyde."

"But you're always happy."

Ken rolled his eyes. He heard the two of us spend more time talking about the book than my health.

"I don't think I'm going to be contributing at all to the sale of your book," Dr. Hoffman commented. At first, I was offended, until I realized that he meant he felt himself to be a boring person and no one would want to read about him.

"Did I tell you that my book is coming out this fall?"

"It is?"

"Yes. I brought my book proposal to an agent and she was very impressed. I still can't believe it."

He asked me to hop up on the examining table and open my mouth. The second the wooden stick was out of my mouth, I brought up the book again.

"I'm calling your colleague across town—the surgeon—Dr. Intelligent."

He put his hands on either side of my neck and maybe the close proximity made me realize what I had just said to him. I looked him straight in the eye (I had no choice) and said, "Oops. I'm not saying *you're* not intelligent."

He laughed.

After the examination was through, I said, "So, you don't want to be called Dr. Happy."

"Are you kidding me? It makes me sound like a psychotherapist prescribing Prozac."

I wonder what they prescribe for schizophrenia.

Every other day I changed my mind about whether or not I wanted to commit to the Marie/Maria Project and lose weight. It sounded like too much work.

Maybe I should just be content with myself the way I was. I recalled a conversation with Dr. Williamson.

"I need to lose a bunch of weight," I told him.

"Why?"

I looked at him in surprise.

"Because I'm overweight."

"And?"

"Everything I've read says that if women have breast cancer and they're overweight, their prognosis isn't that good."

"In other words, you got breast cancer because you gained weight?"

I was confused. Was he saying that it was okay that I was overweight? "Well, maybe it was because I ate too much sugar and..."

"Hold it right there, Maria." He knit his brows together and pulled at his mustache. "People do not get breast cancer because they ate too much sugar. Everyone would have it, then. I had a patient who ate healthy, she was a vegetarian, and she still got breast cancer. She denied all treatment and traveled to Japan to follow an even stricter diet, even though I tried to get her to reconsider chemotherapy."

His whole conversation with me was not helping my case to lose weight at all.

"When I saw her again, her cancer had worsened. It's not always black and white."

* * *

For breakfast one morning, I took out a grapefruit and chopped it in half. It wasn't a big deal, except it finally clicked in my chemo brain that grapefruit was no longer restricted for me; it seems the lowly fruit interferes with certain medications, Lapatinib being one of them, and I hadn't taken that for months.

I took my coveted half of a grapefruit to the living room and turned on the television. *The Today Show* was featuring a blip called "The Ambush Makeover" where they took two dowdy-looking women off the street and transformed them into a sight to behold: highlights, haircuts, fancy clothes, and nice makeup.

As I sat chomping my grapefruit, I thought, "Those women are so lucky. I wish someone would overhaul *me.*"

Then again, I have been ambushed by cancer. I've gone from being a fake blond with lush lashes and eyebrows to being a completely hairless woman with an all-over body rash, back to a gray-haired lady.

Now, if I could just get rid of my obsession with weight loss.

Chapter Twenty-Three
The Hawaii Project

The suitcases were packed except for my two new bras that I had washed in mild soap and hung up to dry. Thankfully, my chemo brain had recuperated enough that I remembered to take the prosthesis out before washing the bras. However, I left it on the dryer by the back door so that I wouldn't forget to take it with me.

It was several hours later while I was in the kitchen getting a drink of water when I heard Isaac (not the little one that prayed for me daily, but Rich's son) ask, "Hey, Jonathan, what's this?" Isaac and Rich planned on spending the night with us since Rich was driving Ken and me to the airport early in the morning.

Oh my. I knew I should have hidden that thing.

Isaac walked around the corner into the kitchen, holding... well, holding my boob.

Jonathan followed him and answered matter-of-factly, "Oh, that's my mom's boob." The next thing I knew, they were *playing* with it. Poking at it, rubbing it, and stroking the fake nipple.

"You boys give me that thing." I took the lump of squishiness and reminded Jonathan, "That thing cost $500 and is not a toy." It wasn't even a toy for Ken. However, it would prove to be a toy for Rich, Isaac's father, who showed up several hours later and saw the prosthesis, which had by now moved to the dining room table.

"Hey, what's this?" Rich echoed Isaac's earlier question. "Oh, a boobie. Hey, Maria, can I play with this tonight? You don't need it until tomorrow, right? I'm lonely."

"Rich, only you could say that and get away with it," I replied.

"Hey, Ken, can I play with your wife's boob?" Now, that's not something you hear every day.

The next morning, I packed one of the dry bras into the suitcase, put the prosthesis back into the bra I planned on wearing, and off we went to celebrate our anniversary, seemingly on the other side of the world.

I determined that I was going to exercise and eat healthy while I was there. I had purchased a whole new wardrobe, not only because it was my 20th anniversary and I was having major anxiety and self-esteem issues because of the surgery and weight I had gained, but because I had no shorts. I needed shorts for tropical weather. And five sexy new negligees, which were depressing to try on because I was missing half of my body to fit into them properly.

It sure was easy to get motivated on the island of Maui. I was up by 5:30 and on the beach by six the first morning. I had sweats, a tank top, and a pair of tennis shoes on. I was determined to sweat.

Things were going great. I walked and ran along the beach, counting each time I reached the rocks on either end of the sand: one, two, three, four. About halfway through my fourth jaunt, I felt the first twinge of pain. I guess my feet weren't used to the exercise and were making their protest in the form of blisters. I heard them loud and clear then.

I tried to talk myself through the pain. *One more time, make it to five and we'll try harder tomorrow.*

I made the fifth run, but that was it.

I limped all the way back to our room. Sure enough, I had two blisters already.

"Hurry up, Mer, we're going to miss the orientation thing," Ken yelled from the bathroom.

I moaned from the bed, where I was trying to take my tennis shoes off. "What's that again?"

"I don't know, but it's a free breakfast. Let's go."

We walked... well, I hobbled and Ken sprinted—it was free, you know—down to the open "cabana-style" room next to the swimming pool. A group of about 25 had already gathered.

Breakfast consisted of donuts and fruit. Not exactly a big breakfast, but the pineapple was really good.

Our vacation planner was even better. Her name was Lei. She had tanned skin and long, curly black hair, and deep brown eyes. She pointed at the map of Maui displayed at the front of the room. "First of all, Fam-i-lee"—she punctuated each syllable—"if you do nothing else, do the helicopter ride. There are three to choose from."

Family? She was a character. But she was right. I had heard from several other tourists in the short time we had been in Maui that the helicopter ride was the most exciting. What was I thinking? Trying to convince Ken, who was interested only in the free breakfast, to jump into a helicopter? I don't think so.

Oops, Lei had been talking while I was off dreaming about swooping down through the lush rain forests and beautiful flowers of this wonderful place. "If you are into snorkeling," she continued, "the one that I recommend the most is the one to Molokini/Lanai."

The last time I went to Club Lanai 20 years ago as a young bride, I was determined to come back with a tan to avoid all the "Suppose you stayed in your motel room the whole time" comments from my co-workers, and therefore, I had sunburned to a crisp. To top off my torture to an all-new high, I accidentally got suntan lotion in both my eyes and they teared for most of the day while I lay moaning in the hammock. My new husband? He ran all over the island snorkeling, playing volleyball, enjoying a beer by the pool, each event separated by a quick trip to me—his dumb new bride who couldn't seem to get it together on her honeymoon.

"Hey, Ken," I whispered, "it would be fun to try Lanai again and actually snorkel this time."

Lei began explaining some of the other local activities: "Make sure to see a luau. There are several to choose from. My favorite is the Drums of The Pacific. Yes, I used to be a dancer. All I kept from those days is the hair." She paused. "And the coconuts. They're hanging on the wall. Don't touch the coconuts, Family."

Her voice had such a lilting quality to it. I was mesmerized. I was also impressed with how fit she still appeared to be. I didn't have any coconuts hanging on my wall. I would only need one if I did. Maybe I should take up hula dancing. Running along the beach is all fine and dandy, sans blisters, but it would be fun to add to my exercise repertoire.

I wondered if coconuts come in size G.

"Submarine rides are another option," the lilting voice continued.

I had a word. Claustrophobia.

"Okay, Family, the harrowing car ride to Hana. People have driven off the cliff there, so make sure you're aware of that."

What? We could go off a cliff and not return home? Maybe we should rethink this trip to Hana. I don't think death and vacation should ever be used in the same sentence.

Lei pointed to the map again. "Parasailing." She turned back to the crowd. "You can't do this activity if you are pregnant or have had back surgery in the past year."

Did I dare ask if having your breast removed was on the same plane as having back surgery?

"Okay, Family, you have heard all of the fun things to do. I'm here and Jeff is back there. We can book any fun things you want to do. First, we do our drawing for some free stuff, good stuff, Family, for you to do. If you no like your prize, you switch with someone else, okay, Family? You still clap for others who win, though, no?"

We all nodded our heads like the good family members that we were.

Ken took out our ticket and put it in his lap, a hopeful look on his face. I was hopeful, too, but not as much as Ken. We never won anything.

"Okay, number 04968."

A young pregnant woman raised her hand; the rest of us, the jealous family members, clapped, simply because we said we would. The woman made her way to the front of the room.

Lei handed her a certificate. "You won a ten-minute foot massage from Louise." She eyed the recipient up and down. "You gonna need that, girlfriend."

I needed that too, girlfriend. Darn. Like I said, we never won anything.

"Okay. Now, number 04284."

An older couple stood up while we all clapped again.

"You've won a 'Buy one, get one free' ticket for the Road to Hana."

Darn again. I know Ken was probably the most interested in this trip. Back home, he had told me he wanted to go to Hana. He had planned on driving it himself until Lei started mentioning how much nicer it was to have someone else drive you so that you could concentrate on the beautiful sights rather than the road. Not driving *off* the road, that was still my biggest concern.

"Next number is 04277."

"Ken," I whispered again, "all the numbers are 04-something. Our number starts with 05. I just know we're going to be left in the dust." Boy, for being such a self-described optimistic person, I sure was down in the mouth this morning. Maybe it was the wretched blisters that were putting me in a funk.

Another lucky couple stood up to collect their "Buy one, get one free" snorkeling prize.

"Okay, now is time to book your fun activities, Family. First come, first served," Lei said.

I scrambled to check the price list. I knew Ken wasn't going to go for half the stuff I had marked on my wish list. Don't get me wrong, it's not like he always says no, it's just that the Dutch, practical blood runs a little thicker in his veins. The helicopter rides ranged in price from $249 per person to $350 per person.

"Which ones are you looking at?" I timidly asked Ken.

"I want to do the Road to Hana," Ken answered me.

I knew it.

"I wouldn't mind doing the snorkeling thing, either."

Boy, did I have him pegged or what?

I decided to take the plunge. "What do you think about that helicopter thing?"

"Did you see the price?" he asked me.

Of course I saw the price. I was just hoping for a miracle; out of all the things that Lei had described, that was the one thing I wanted to do the most. "Yeah, I saw the price," I admitted.

"That would be over 500 bucks."

Well, when he said it like that.

"Susie gave us a $100 Visa card for my end-of-chemo birthday bash. We could use that for the luau the night of our anniversary. That's what she bought for our honeymoon, remember? It would be nice to use that for the luau of our second honeymoon."

"Maybe." He didn't look as convinced as I was that this was a good idea. The glaze over his eyes was my first clue. The one-word answer was my second clue.

Jeff walked over to where we sat. "Are there any questions over here?"

"Yeah, got any way to make a lot of cash quick?" is what I wanted to say. What I said instead was, "We're just looking." All I needed was for a pushy salesman to kill any chance at all of my convincing Ken that the helicopter ride was the chance of a lifetime.

Jeff sat back down and I noticed an older couple plunk down large amounts of cash to do it all. We still had private tuition and medical bills to think about.

Ken stood up.

I nudged him. "Make sure we get Lei," I advised. I don't know what made me say it. Jeff seemed nice enough, but I really wanted to talk to Lei. Maybe it was the lilting voice. Before we made it to Lei, however, the couple next to us—the pregnant couple who had won the free foot massage—came up to us.

"Hey, you guys want this free foot massage?"

A free helicopter would be better. Would that be rude to say?

"Sure," Ken agreed, taking the winning ticket. "Do you guys want this snorkeling coupon? Some guy just handed it to me."

"That would be great," the husband answered. "By the way, we have a ticket for Hana, too. Do you want it?"

"Yes." Ken took the proffered ticket and handed it to me.

"Don't you two want to use it?" I asked.

"Some other couple just gave it to us," the pregnant woman entered the conversation. "We won't use it. My husband wants to drive it himself. It's just too expensive, even with the coupon."

I needed to rethink this mentality that we never won anything. I had two coupons in my hand, one for a massage and one for a free trip to Hana, that said otherwise.

Finally, we found ourselves in front of Lei.

"So, Family," she said in her cheerful voice, "what partying are *we* going to do?"

"I want to do the helicopter ride, but we're thinking it's too expensive," I began. I needed to put it out there for her right away.

"Okay, first we take out our schedule. You're here for ten days? Wow."

"Trust me. I'm still pinching myself."

Lei took out a piece of paper with a calendar on it. She wrote down all the days we were going to be there.

Ken jumped in. "We know we want to do the Road to Hana." I slid the coupon across the desk.

"Would you like to do that tomorrow?" Lei asked.

"Sure."

"Okay, what else we want to do, Family?"

I let Ken lead the conversation. "We'd like to do the luau on the 25th. That's our anniversary."

"Good choice, good choice. Congratulations. How many years, Family?"

"Twenty. Isn't that exciting? I think we should hop in

that helicopter to celebrate, what do you think, Lei?" I asked eagerly.

"The Molokini/Lanai snorkeling... what day could we do that?" Ken cut in.

"How about Tuesday?"

Ken nodded.

"About that helicopter ride," I shamelessly plugged, "is there a way we can change the 'Buy one, get one free' Hana trip to a 'Buy one, get one free' helicopter ride?" I didn't want this opportunity to slip through my fingers.

"No, but do you know anyone that has AARP? It would be ten percent off."

"No, I don't." Ten percent... I wanted about a thousand percent off, because that's what it would take to change Ken's mind on the whole subject.

I turned to Ken. "When the book comes out this fall and we sell a million copies, can we do the helicopter ride then?"

"Yeah, we'll do it then." He smiled at me, but I'm sure he wanted to wring my neck by this time.

"You wrote a book?" Lei asked politely.

"Yes, about having cancer. It's called *Cancer Is A Funny Thing*."

"That's awesome."

"It's going to end with us being here in Maui."

"Oh!" she exclaimed. "You need to end it with you in the helicopter. I can see it now, Family." She gazed up toward the ceiling, her arms spread out in dramatic fashion. "A nice picture of you both flying through the air..."

Lei and I were on the same page.

She leaned across the desk and said quietly, "I can pull a

few strings and your helicopter ride would be ten percent off." She showed us the corrected price.

"What if we cancelled everything else and just did the helicopter ride?" I asked. I was beginning to grasp at straws. Ken was strangely quiet.

She gave us the price difference again.

Ken stood. "I'm going to the room to get the credit card."

I don't think he could stand the pressure, especially with two women breathing down his neck. I began to feel guilty. I didn't want to put the guy into the poorhouse. He had been through enough over the past year.

While Ken was gone, Lei leaned back in her chair and said, "Marie, my mother died of cancer. Your book will really help people. This island is very healing. The ocean, too. Very healing."

"I'm finding it very relaxing here, that's for sure."

"I meant it when I said the helicopter ride would be a very good ending to your book."

This woman got me. Yes, it was her job to sell, but she had also talked us out of a few things, which I admired. I could see it in my mind's eye, the ending to the book. "You know, Lei, it took me five hours for me to convince Ken just to become members of this time-share. I don't think I'm going to change his mind on this whole helicopter thing."

"Sorry about not helping in that department," she apologized.

"You did fine."

Ken walked into the room and sat down next to me. "Well, let's do it."

What? Were my ears deceiving me?

“Cancel everything and do just the helicopter ride, you mean?” I asked.

“No, all of it.”

Lei was already typing. She probably thought she’d better hurry before her customer changed his mind and scurried away.

“Yippee!” I yelled into the soft breeze flowing through the cabana.

Chapter Twenty-Four
Wedding Anniversary

Three days before our anniversary, we were up by six and out in the parking lot by seven. We were waiting for the van that would take us to Hana. By 7:20, still no van.

"I'm going to go use the bathroom in the lobby," I told Ken. He stayed outside.

I was almost done in the bathroom when Ken knocked furiously on the door. "The bus is here. You're the last one." Murphy's Law. Wait for 20 minutes and the bus won't come until you're sitting on the pot.

The van had 12 people on it already. Ken and I made 14.

The driver yelled into his microphone, "My name is Ed. We have one more couple to pick up and then we're on our way."

"Are you excited for this?" I asked Ken.

"Yeah. I'm glad we didn't take the rental car and we can sit back and relax. Aren't you looking forward to it?"

"Heck, yeah. I just hope we don't go off the road." I couldn't get Lei's words out of my head. Suddenly, I could have sworn I felt a raindrop fall on my head. I knew that was impossible since we were inside a vehicle. A few more drops landed on my head.

I shifted over in my seat, closer to Ken.

"What's the problem?" Ken asked me.

"I feel dripping water landing on me."

Ken looked up. "I think it's the coil of the air conditioner. That will stain your clothes."

"Perfect. These are all new clothes and you know how long it's been since I've done that." It was going to be a long trip.

"You can go sit by that guy up there," Ken said.

"Why would I spend eight hours next to a stranger instead of sitting by you?" Guess the second honeymoon was over.

"Well, I'm telling you that stuff is going to stain your clothes."

What happened to Ken? He sure was a bit grumpy this morning. *He* could go sit by that stranger.

Drip. Drip. Drip.

"Hey, Ed," Ken yelled, "the air conditioner is dripping water back here."

"I'll see what I can do about getting a new bus for us," Ed quickly replied.

We swung by the tiny airport and pulled into a shady area. "If you need to use the bathroom, now is your chance," Ed advised. "We'll wait here for the other van. They're bringing another one over."

I cringed. I hoped people weren't mad that I was delaying the trip. No one seemed to be disturbed by my complaining. Especially when we saw the replacement bus. It was a much newer Ford with more room, and more importantly, a new air conditioner.

Off we went. Boy, the brochures weren't kidding when they said that there were over 600 switchbacks. I was beginning to feel a little sick to my stomach. I counted myself lucky, though, because the man three seats up from me, the one Ken wanted me to sit by, I might add, wasn't so lucky. For two reasons. First, he puked. Everywhere. Second, as if that wasn't bad enough, his wife across the aisle began to slap his arm and berate him loudly in front of everyone.

Lucky me that I didn't sit next to him, or I would have joined him in the vomiting fest.

"Yeah, Jim Nabors and Kris Kristofferson have property around here," Ed explained. I don't know how he stayed on the road. He must have been taking the curves at 40 miles per hour.

Please stay on the road.

"Woody Harrelson... that's his driveway right there." Ed waved his arm to the right. "Pat Benatar lives around here, also. By the way, Oprah Winfrey owns property around here. She promised the locals she'll never build here but keep it untouched the way it is now."

I almost belted out, "Oprah's my friend. I'm going to

be on her show when my book comes out and she gets a chance to read it. Got the dress picked out and everything." Thankfully, I refrained myself and kept my mouth shut for once.

"Charles Lindbergh came to Maui because of his friend Sam Pryor. Sam had six gibbon monkeys that he loved so much, he took them everywhere with him: traveling, to the store; he even took them in church with him. Those six monkeys are buried at the place that we're going to.

"Charles Lindbergh loved Maui so much that he told his wife, Ann, that he wanted to be buried here. After his death, Ann was so upset she swore she'd never set foot on this island again, and she never has."

"I plan on coming here again. What about you, Ken?" I asked. I was so glad we were able to sit together on this eight-hour trek.

"Yeah, after your book sells millions of copies, we're coming again. I want to bring the whole family."

"Sounds good to me."

* * *

On May 25, the actual date of our anniversary, Ken and I went to Sugar Beach Resort where we had spent our honeymoon. We walked around the grounds and onto the white sandy beach.

We held hands as we walked along the shore.

"It's so weird to be here again, isn't it, Ken? I'm still pinching myself. Twenty years, can you believe it?"

"Sometimes I can and sometimes I can't."

"What would you change?"

"You getting cancer."

"Fat chance of that. Besides, it's had its blessings. You realize we wouldn't be here if it weren't for me getting cancer, right?"

"I don't know about that."

"It's true, Ken. We would have waited for our 25th anniversary."

That night, we attended the Drums of the Pacific Luau and had our picture taken against the sunset. I planned to take the photo home and put it in a frame to celebrate another 20 years together.

Chapter Twenty-Five
The Helicopter Ride

"I have to blog a few more times before the end of this month," I told Ken in a panic.

"What difference does it make how many times you blog?"

"I committed to entering 15 per month," I answered.

"Committed to whom?"

"Myself."

"What are you going to blog about?" he prompted.

"I don't know. I'll think of something."

I didn't want to admit it, but for all my bravado at our meeting with Lei, I was getting a bit nervous for this helicopter ride. It had sounded so glamorous at the time.

I sat in front of the computer in the downstairs lobby

of the condo, my fingers poised above the screen. Within minutes, I had a blog:

Translating Hawaiian Words

Big Beach

Beautiful beach, clothing mandatory.

Little Beach

Another beach, clothing optional.

Humuhumunukunukuapua'a

Beautiful fish with the snout of a pig.

Marie "Malia" de Haan

Grown woman leaving her bathing suit on with the heart of a big, fat chicken.

I still couldn't believe that we had visited Little Beach. It was Sunday night and there was supposed to be a Circle of Fire and drum music. What it really was, was a circle of crazy people running around naked.

I clutched my blanket nervously and followed Ken down to the ocean shore. I sat down, turned to view the ocean, and instead, got a full view of an old, wrinkled man without a stitch of clothes on.

There was no nervousness about him. He slinked along the sand and began to do various Yoga positions. Why was it that the people who should leave their clothes on didn't, and the ones that—

What was I saying? All of these people should have been

keeping their clothes on. I knew I was going to do so.

The next thing I knew, the man in front of us had an admirer. Another older gentleman came over with a camera and began to take pictures. Very close-up pictures. I backed up on the blanket, keeping out of the photographer's viewfinder.

All of a sudden I caught a waft of something familiar. "Ken," I nudged him, "I smell marijuana. Can you smell it?"

"Yes. I'm sure it's all over here. Did you know they call it Maui Wowie?"

"I think I heard Lei mention that the other day at our breakfast orientation. Speaking of that, Ken, are you ready for our helicopter ride Thursday?"

"I'm really excited for it, aren't you?"

"Uh... I'm thinking maybe it's pretty high up there."

"Mer, you'll be fine."

"Is it me or is that man in front of us getting closer and closer to us?"

Time to go.

The next day, we visited the larger beach, Big Beach. Ken was determined we were going to relax in the sun all day.

First, there were the shore breaks. No matter how many times I tried to go wading in the ocean, I kept getting knocked off my feet and slammed into the sand. The fourth time the waves took me off my feet, I think I got sand in my tonsils.

Second, there were the umbrellas. No matter how many times Ken tried to set one up over me so I wouldn't burn, it would collapse over my head.

Third, there was my sunburn. It happened in ten minutes.

Frustrated, I stood up. "Ken, I don't care if you want to relax here all day. I'm done with this wretched beach, and I want to go back to our condo right now." Not one of my finer moments.

I did, however, tell Ken later, "Hey, I got a good one." We were sitting on the couch in our condo eating coconut gelato and watching *The Secret Life of Bees*. "Maui Marijuana... Maui Wowie. The sunburn I got today? Maui Owie."

Before I knew it, the day of the helicopter ride arrived.

I clutched the roll of Mentos in my hand and even a few pieces of ginger left from the boat ride back from Lanai. Fat lot of good that ginger did me there. About five of us sat at the back of the boat, feeding our lunch to the fish over the side.

Why, oh why exactly did I try so hard to talk Ken into this idea of going in a small aircraft and hurtling through the air? I hate heights.

It sounded so romantic at the time. Now, all I wanted to do was stay here on solid ground.

We entered the air-conditioned waiting area of Hawaiian Helicopters.

The first thing I noticed was a man lying down on one of the lobby couches. Great.

The woman who checked us in said, "Yeah, he didn't do too well on the ride."

There was still time to turn back.

"Just how does a helicopter ride compare to say, car sickness or boat rides back from Lanai?" I asked the ticket-taker. Her name was Lelani.

"It's not too bad. Once in a while, people get sick. There are bags on the helicopter."

Bags. That just meant that they were counting on people to be sick. Oh, what had I gotten myself into?

Ken and I sat and watched the video that was currently showing, *Visions From Hawaii.* The scenery was spectacular. I just hoped I could enjoy myself and actually see it rather than the inside of a barf bag.

As time marched relentlessly on toward the 2:30 mark, a few more people straggled into the waiting area.

For some reason, I thought Ken and I were going to have the helicopter all to ourselves. With the pilot, of course. For the price we paid, I would think so, but apparently, we were going to be with strangers. It was hard enough to vomit in front of my husband, but I didn't want to do it in front of someone I didn't know. What was I saying? I didn't want to vomit, period.

2:15. A nice young couple came in.

"Okay," Lelani announced, "we have a safety video to show you, so I would please ask for your undivided attention."

You didn't need to tell me twice.

"...Click the seatbelt securely... never, ever walk toward the back of the helicopter where the blades..."

Will chop off your head, I thought. *I hope I'm not nervous enough to do something like that. Hopefully, someone will stop me in time.*

"There are comfort bags..."

Comfort bags? Is that what they were calling them

nowadays?

"We'll be boarding in a few moments. Are there any questions?"

"How often do people get sick on these trips?"

"You should be fine."

I noticed the couple was holding hands and bowing their heads. It looked like they might be praying. They were probably praying for me not to puke all over them. I couldn't agree with them more and sent up a small prayer myself.

When they were done praying, they stood up and walked over to where Ken and I stood in front of the window.

"My name is Carlos and this is my wife, Anna."

"Where are you from?" Ken asked.

"Melbourne."

"I thought that was an Australian accent," Ken answered. "I'm Ken. This is Marie."

"Where are you from?"

"Seattle area."

"Cool. We're here on our honeymoon."

"We're here on our 20th anniversary," I finally contributed to the conversation.

"We'd love to come back here sometime for our anniversary."

"Don't wait twenty years, though," I admonished, like some old grandmother. "It took cancer to make us come five years earlier than we expected, so make sure you come sooner."

"Isn't that the truth," Anna commented. "You never know what life throws you."

"Okay, everyone," Lelani announced, "line up in this

order: Carlos, Anna, Ken, Marie."

I realized that I would be last, which most likely meant that I would be sitting in the back seat. I whispered my question. "Is it worse in the back seat for motion sickness, like in a car?"

"Not really," Lelani answered. What she really meant was, "Shut up, lady, quit asking me about your motion sickness, and get your ass on that helicopter."

Our pilot walked in. His name was David.

Carlos and Anna sat in the front seat to David's left; I sat behind them, while Ken sat directly behind the pilot. To my right, a big space separated us—probably a good thing, or I might have scarred Ken's arms with my fingernails.

Soon, we were off the ground. Five feet. So far, so good. I tried to calculate how long it took me to feel sick on the Molokini/Lanai boat rides. It was toward the end of the day. That was in my favor.

I looked at my watch. 2:45. That meant the countdown to 3:30 was on.

It was smoother than I thought.

Before I knew it, we were flying over the ocean above the parasailers. I began to snap pictures with my Canon Rebel.

The water was so blue-green in spots.

I turned to look at Ken. He had a look of complete bliss on his face. To prove it, he caught my eye and gave me the thumbs up sign.

It was too hard to talk above the sound of the engine.

David's voice came over the loudspeaker. "Where you folks from?"

"Marie and I are from the Seattle area," Ken replied.

"We're from Melbourne," Carlos said.

"Down there is where they filmed Jurassic Park," David told us. "It's a beautiful place. Now, if you notice the smoke in the air, that's from the Kilauea Volcano. It's been erupting for 27 years."

"Twenty-seven years?" Ken asked over the loudspeaker. "Where is that?"

"It's on the Big Island."

A few moments later, we swooped seemingly straight down the side of a cliff. I almost choked on my Mento. I felt like I was in one of those bad dreams where the elevator becomes loose from the cable holding it.

"These are the highest sea cliffs in the world."

No kidding. I'm about to lose my lunch.

The view was spectacular. I had never seen anything quite like it. I snapped picture after picture. I tapped Ken on the arm. He gave me a huge grin, which I captured on my camera. I smiled back. I was giddy with happiness.

Before I knew it, the ride was over.

If I could get through this helicopter ride, skyrocketing over the highest sea cliffs in the world back down to solid ground, surely I can weather the teetering at the edge of the cliff that my life has become.

Breast cancer has forced me to stand at the precipice, plummeting down toward the depths of despair. But I will not be bowled over by my illness. I know, somehow, that I will make it.

Solid ground. It's always a good thing.

And as my little friend Isaac prays daily: "Heal Maria!"

Acknowledgements

Stephanie Chandler

Thank you for your patience with me as a new author. You made the experience quite painless.

You are aptly named Authority Publishing because you know what you're doing.

Amberly Finarelli

You're a great editor. I appreciated your comments and insight. Thank you for helping me to choose my words carefully in telling this story.

Andrea Hurst

Thank you for believing in me and telling me to "go copyright that title." This book would never have seen the light of day if it had not been for your encouraging words, your gentle guidance, and the opportunity to join your writing group every week.

Just Write

Thank you for being there for me every week, telling me I looked great in my scarves (and no eyelashes) and laughing every time I read a blog post out loud to you. If I can write a book, any of you can, too.

Susie Spaeth

You are a true friend. Thank you for reading over the first couple chapters and telling me I had a "bestseller on my hands." And the party you threw for me to celebrate the end of chemotherapy? Way beyond the call of duty. I still owe you a birthday dinner.

Debbie Sparks

You're another great driver and I loved all our shopping trips together. The time we bought the hope chest for Adriana and you stopped the semi-pro football player on the sidewalk to load it into the car was my all-time favorite.

Laurie Top

You're an awesome webmaster. You have a gift for all things computer and the patience of Job in dealing with me and my incessant questions.

Ria VanDyken

Thank you for all the encouraging emails you sent me and the occasional phone calls. You scraped me off the floor more than once. I am thankful that the Lord has kept you cancer free all these years and pray that He continues to bless you in your life.

Tami Vogel

I feel I cannot do anything without your prior approval. Thank you so much for all the driving you did to and from chemotherapy. Most of all, I treasure our long-term friendship. Without you, life would not be worth living.

and

My Caregivers

I thank God for you. You saved my life.

Resource Guide

All of the products listed below are ones that I have personally used.

Living Earth Herbs

"Sassy Sensual Oil"

I used this oil for problems associated with neuropathy caused by Taxol as detailed in the book.

Certain oils are compatible with condoms and some are not, so please be sure to ask.

(360) 734-3207

www.livingearthherbs.com

Hawaiian ScentSations

"Mo Bettah Cream"

When I was in Maui with my husband, I got sunburned on top of all the other skin issues I already had because of the Taxol/Lapatinib and Herceptin.

This lotion was made without chemicals. (I figured enough chemicals had entered my body with the chemotherapy.) It smells wonderful and is the best lotion I've come across.

www.hawaiianscentsations.com

TriVita

"Stress Protection Pack"

I used Sublingual B-12 and Adaptogen Plus throughout my treatment as both of these products helped me with stress and low energy levels. Cancer is definitely stressful and fatiguing.

Mention code 10854847.

1-800-991-7116

www.trivita.com

Tropical Traditions

"Gold Label Standard Virgin Coconut Oil"

I used coconut oil on my skin when the Lapatinib rash got really out of control and it was very soothing. I also used it in place of Vagasil or similar products when Herceptin caused me to have issues. I plan to use it if I ever need it for vaginal dryness in place of chemical substitutes for these problems.

www.tropicaltraditions.com

Wayside Wisteria Theme Gardens

"Handmade, blank greeting cards"

When I was first diagnosed with breast cancer, I was immediately approached by well-meaning friends and family with 600-page health books that I was pressed upon to read, and emailed by those same friends to partake of the "Maple Syrup and Baking Soda" cure and the "asparagus diet."

I did not want to read a book to hear about how much *more* guilty I should feel because of the vegetables I didn't eat or the sugar I did eat. I also did not want to eat maple syrup (except on oatmeal) or bucket-loads of asparagus. If I was going to eat baking soda, it was going to be in the form of a cake.

What I wanted was to read the cards that poured in. I treasured the sentiments that people wrote on those cards.

www.waysidewisteria.com

15392 Allen West Road, Bow Washington 98232

1-888-372-2804

The author assumes no legal liability for the above products. Please use at your own risk.